iPhc

MW01241158

A Comprehensive Guide to Help You
Learn about All Your iPhone Features
and Their Uses

By

Albrecht Meyer

Under no circumstances will any legal responsibility or blame be held against the publisher for any reparation, damages, or monetary loss due to the information herein, either directly or indirectly.

Respective author(s) own all copyrights not held by the publisher.

The information herein is offered for informational purposes solely and is universal as so. The presentation of the information is without contract or any type of guarantee assurance.

The trademarks that are used are without any consent, and the publication of the trademark is without permission or backing by the trademark owner. All trademarks and brands within this book are for clarifying purposes only and are the owned by the owners themselves, not affiliated with this document.

Table of Contents

Introduction

In 2019, Apple launched three new iPhones i.e. iPhone 11, iPhone 11 Pro and iPhone 11 Pro Max which were quite similar to the previous year's phones. The striking change in these phones was the enhanced features of camera. All three iPhones got a brand new ultra-wide camera allowing users to capture stunning tight-space shots and landscape photos. In 2019, Apple offered users what they had wanted for years, which was slightly thicker phones with large batteries. It elevated the Pro and the Pro Max to go to the top of battery life rankings. The other masterstroke was the Night Mode feature, which is a new camera function that allowed the iPhone users to combine a long exposure picture with many others through an easy process while capturing fantastic images in very dim light.

The iPhone 11 Pro Max is the Tech Giant's most excellent flagship smartphone. It features a 6.5-inch display Super Retina XDR, up to 512 GB of storage, and A13 Bionic chipset. It is the first iPhone to have a triple-camera. Apart from the main wide-angle and the Telephoto-camera, there is an ultra-wide camera.

For photo processing, the Deep Fusion function utilizes the advanced learning and Chipset's Neural Engine to offer pixel optimization for better detail, textures, a dynamic range, and lower noise in final images.

This book will prove to be a complete guide to learn some fantastic features of the iPhone 11 Pro Max. In the first chapter of this book, you will learn about the history of the iPhone. It will also discuss how it evolved and what Apple did in terms of adding more advanced technology and features with every new iPhone in the line. Chapter two will help you learn how to set up your iPhone 11 Pro Max. You will get to know some crucial things while using your iPhone, like backing up your data from your previous phone, activating your Apple and Face ID, iCloud, and some useful tips regarding iOS 13 to make the best out of your iPhone and much more. In chapter three, we will see what Siri is and what it can offer to you. You will also learn how to use Siri to make the most out of this fantastic function.

In chapter four, we will learn about Messages and Email settings in your iPhone 11 Pro Max. You can now enjoy amazing features in SMS, MMS, iMessaging, and Email to view and share your images and videos to another person and on social media.

Chapter five will introduce you to the various features and settings regarding calls and contacts in your iPhone 11 Pro Max. Chapter six will discuss some cool features that the camera in the iPhone 11 Pro Max has. As you move forward in this book, you will be introduced to different tabs available in the App Store, serving the users' various needs. You will then learn to install and uninstall apps, along with some App Store settings, to fully benefit from the App Store functions.

Chapter eight covers the features and settings of Notes and Reminders Apps in the iPhone 11 Pro Max. The last chapters of the book discuss the features and settings of the iTunes App and the Books App in the iPhone 11 Pro Max. We will also learn some tips on tackling some issues for the smooth working of these apps. Apart from that, Apple has added some new features in the iPhone 11 Pro Max with iOS 13. This book will help you to master those features and settings also. In short, you will have a complete user guide of your iPhone 11 Pro Max in the form of this book.

Chapter 1: iPhone 11 Pro Max at a Glance

This chapter will take you to a journey of the history of the iPhone. It will discuss how it has evolved over time and what Apple has done to add more advanced and fantastic technology and features with every new iPhone in the line. Apple has always tried to give its users the best experience of having an iPhone in their hands. With the iPhone 11 Pro Max, Apple has succeeded in doing the same.

1.1 Evolution of iPhone Through the Course of History

After Apple introduced the first-generation iPhone in 2007, it created the next one that had 3G internet connectivity. Apple has released twenty iPhones over the years, including iPhone 3, iPhone 4, iPhone 5, iPhone S, and the iPhone Plus models. Next comes the iPhone 11 line and the iPhone SE. Let's look at Apple's iPhone evolution over time:

iPhone: 2007

There was not as much data to put on that iPhone. It had no App Store. The good thing was it had access to the internet. It had 128 MB of memory space with a 2.0-megapixel camera.

iPhone 3G: 2008

It was very close to the original iPhone. But it had an App Store with its 3G connectivity which meant fast access to the internet.

iPhone 3GS: 2009

Apple created 32 GB storage in the iPhone 3GS. The camera got 3 MP and also added video recording. Voice Control was also added to it.

iPhone 4: 2010

The iPhone 4 was the pioneer in having a front-facing camera. It got a Retina Display. It had 512 MB memory, it means that it was much better in handling much more than the iPhone 3GS.

iPhone 4S: 2011

The camera on this iPhone went from 5 MP to 8 MP. Apple introduced the 64 GB storage with a memory of 512 MB. Siri was introduced on this iPhone.

iPhone 5: 2012

The camera on this iPhone stayed the same. Memory was boosted to 1 GB. Apple introduced the Lightning connector and big screen on this iPhone.

iPhone 5s & iPhone 5c: 2013

The iPhone 5c had four different colors. The iPhone 5s introduced dual flash, Touch ID, and the slow-motion video. It also included the M7 motion coprocessor.

iPhone 6 & 6 Plus: 2014

The internal specifications of iPhone 6 were similar to the iPhone 5s. The big difference was a larger screen and even a much larger size in 6 Plus. The Retina Display was HD with 128 GB of storage.

iPhone 6s & 6s Plus: 2015

Apple upgraded the iPhone 6s. The camera went from 8 MP to 12 MP, and the memory went from 1 GB to 2 GB. Apple introduced the iPhone 6s 7000 series aluminum Last after iPhone 6s with 3D Touch.

iPhone SE: 2016

It had all fantastic internal specs of the previous model with a small package and also without 3D Touch. The iPhone SE was introduced so most people could afford it because of its low price.

iPhone 7 & 7 Plus: 2016

Apple finally introduced storage up to 256 GB. Apple introduced a new Jet Black color. The iPhone 7 Plus had a dual camera with improved Portrait mode and Zoom feature.

iPhone 8 & 8 Plus: 2017

The iPhone 8 and 8 Plus are famous for wireless charging and the glass cover on the iPhone's backside. There were upgraded tools for filtering and editing photos.

iPhone X: 2017

The iPhone X introduced an extra front-facing camera to take selfies in Portrait mode.

iPhone XS & XS Max: 2018

Apple introduced the XS and XS Max at the Steve Jobs Theater. Both iPhone models had a front-facing camera. They had a Super Retina HD display and the A12 bionic chip that increased the processing power.

iPhone XR: 2018

This model was cheaper among the new ones. It was smaller than the XS and XS Max in size. This model got the front-facing camera and had more colors than the previous models.

iPhone 11: 2019

This model is the least expensive and most popular of the company's annual line. The device has a 6.1-inch Liquid Retina display. It is available in six colors. The most exciting feature was the second camera on the back, both having 12 MP and also offering ultra-wide and wide lenses.

iPhone 11 Pro: 2019

It is a perfect iPhone option for a smaller phone with a top-of-the-line display, a 5.8-inch Super Retina XDR display, and three 12 MP HDR camera lenses.

iPhone 11 Pro Max: 2019

It is Apple's most expensive and largest phone in 2019. The display is sized at 6.5-inches. It features the three-lens cameras and the same color choices as iPhone 11.

iPhone SE (second generation): 2020

The iPhone SE features Apple's most expensive iPhone features with advanced camera systems having Portrait mode, high-definition video, long battery life, and wireless charging capability.

1.2 Technical Specifications of iPhone 11 Pro Max

Physical Specifications

iPhone 11 Pro Max has dimensions of 158 x 77.8 x 8.1 mm and 226 g of weight. It also got an IP rating of IP68 for protection against dust and water.

Screen and keys

iPhone 11 Pro Max has a Super Retina XDR display with 6.5 inches screen size, and 1242 x 2688 pixels resolution.

SIM

The SIM type in the iPhone 11 Pro Max is Nano-SIM and eSIM.

Memory

The iPhone 11 Pro Max storage capacity is 64 GB, 256 GB, and 512 GB with 4 GB RAM.

Connectivity

It has got Bluetooth, 5, A2DP, LE, and 802.11 dual-band Wi-Fi with NFC and GPS systems.

Networks

iPhone 11 Pro Max has 2G, 3G, and 4G networks.

Sensors

iPhone 11 Pro Max has Accelerometer, Gyroscope, Compass, Barometer sensors.

Operating system

iPhone 11 Pro Max has the operating system iOS 13.0. iOS 13 that gives a very bold new look along with some significant updates to your apps, which you use on a daily basis.

It gives you new ways to protect your privacy. It improves the entire system on your phone that makes your iPhone more fun to use.

Accessibility

The accessibility features of iPhone 11 Pro Max are useful for people, especially with some disabilities, to get the most out of iPhone 11 Pro max features. It has built-in support for hearing, vision, learning, and mobility. It includes features like Voice Control, Zoom, Siri and Dictation, Magnifier, Switch Control, AssistiveTouch, Speak Screen, and many more.

Battery

Battery type of iPhone 11 Pro Max is Non-removable Li-Ion 3969 mAh.

Tethering

iPhone 11 Pro Max has a USB and Wi-Fi hotspot in it.

Size and Weight

The iPhone 11 Pro Max is a little bit wider and taller than its predecessor, but it is 18 grams heavier. It might require two hands to go to the top of the screen. It is one of the few phones that are made of stainless steel. It is definitely more durable than aluminum.

The midnight green color is a fantastic change of pace from the regular gold, space grey, and silver. The 6.5-inch screen is fully wrapped with bezels that seem slim while looking at it. The iPhone 11 Pro Max's screen looks modern and elegant.

Camera

It has three cameras, a wide-angle camera with 12 MP and f/1.8, 26mm, a Telephoto camera with 12 MP, f/2.0, 52 mm, and an ultra-wide camera with 12 MP and f/2.4, 13mm. The front camera has 12 MP and f/2.2, 23mm. Video can be recorded at 2160p, 1080p, and HDR. It has a built-in flash, music player, and a stereo speaker. There is a "Night Mode" feature for low-light photos in iPhone 11 Pro Max. It is also a new feature named "Semantic Rendering" that captures several underexposed photos before tapping the shutter button. The image you want when you press the button and an overexposed image after that to balance out the lighting. It later merges them.

The camera in this phone understands specific parts of the picture, like a flower or a face, and applies individual Smart HDR improvements to those particular areas rather than a whole blanket for the entire photo.

All of this can be viewed through a triple-camera system. Photos captured during the daytime deliver natural colors, sometimes with a little warm tone. Details in the image are extremely strong, and toggling between these lenses feels like a smooth move. The telephoto lens in this phone offers more detail in low-light conditions.

Gestures & Motion

You can control iPhone 11 Pro Max through your hand movements. This feature is impressive. For example:

To Open an App

o Choose an app to open it. Go back to the home screen.

o By swiping left or right, you can see other screens. The dots right above "Dock" show the number of home screens and which one you are using and viewing right now.

To See or Close a Running App

o Swipe up from the bottom of your phone's screen without removing the finger.

o Swipe right or left to view more. To go to another app, select that app.

o If a particular app is not running correctly, force it to shut down by choosing and dragging that app to the top of your phone's screen.

To Zoom In or Out

- Use two fingers on your phone's screen, move those fingers apart a bit to zoom in, and bring them closer to zoom out.
- You can also double-tap a picture to zoom in, or double-tap one more time to zoom out.

To View Notifications

In order to view the most recent "Push Notifications," you need to swipe down from the top of your phone's screen.

To Move an App

- Tap and hold an app from the home screen to the point it starts shaking.
- Drag that app to your desired location.
- Select "Done" to finish.

Screen Icons

Here is the list of screen icons on iPhone 11 Pro Max:

Battery: The battery icon tells about the remaining battery power. The colored section shows the remaining battery power. There is also a battery charging icon that reveals that the battery is being charged.

Network Signal: The network signal icon shows the strength of your network signal. If it shows more lines, the stronger the signal will be.

Flight mode: This icon shows if the flight mode is turned on or off.

Active Data Connection: This icon shows that the data connection is active.

Wi-Fi: This icon tells that the phone is connected to a Wi-Fi network.

Portrait Mode

The amazing change in Portrait mode in this phone is that you can capture an image not with the telephoto lens with an additional feature of using f/1.8 lens as well.

Unlimited Power

Apple's A13 Bionic processor in iPhone 11 Pro Max delivers a 20% faster GPU and CPU performance than the previous model. To launch apps on this iPhone is much more comfortable and the switching between those apps is also convenient.

Fast Updates

This iPhone has iOS 13, and it is excellent. The feature of Dark mode even makes it look more appealing, especially on the screen. It has a faster Face ID as well and swipe typing is available natively.

There are stronger privacy features that offer security. The best part of having this iPhone is getting the latest updates instantly whenever Apple publishes them.

Fantastic Battery Life

The battery life of the iPhone 11 Pro Max is just incredible. It depends on usage as well. Battery life in iPhone 11 Pro Max is about worry-free use and a full day of comfort. Charging speed has been improved in this phone because Apple is packing an 18W fast charger in your iPhone box. It takes almost a little less than one and a half hours to entirely recharge your iPhone from 0 to 100 percent. There is another option of charging that is Wireless charging.

Chapter 2: Setting up your iPhone 11 Pro Max

In this chapter, you will get to learn how to set up your iPhone 11 Pro Max. You will get to know some crucial things if you have unpacked your iPhone like backing up your data from your previous phone, activating your Apple and Face ID, setting iCloud, and some useful tips regarding iOS 13 to make the best out of your iPhone, and much more.

2.1 Backup your Previous iPhone

You realize that you have downloaded a ton of apps throughout the years. You have an iPhone now; at that point, make sure that you do not lose your data. There will be endless iOS or app inclinations that you set up or adjusted, and you can possibly recollect them when they are no more. Spare yourself the aggravation of finding an app, or the login info used by you for your work. You can do this by backing up your old iPhone before you even switch on the upgraded one. To reinforce your iPhone, you can either use iCloud or iTunes.

Nowadays, among all the available choices, you will likely find that iCloud is the most advantageous.

In any case, however, you must have enough space accessible for the reinforcement. If you do not have space on that, you need to advise the Mac to spare it elsewhere. When you are using iCloud, it's simpler and harder to deal with being out of space. That is because truly, you have just got one alternative. If your current iPhone reveals that you need more stockpiling to store the reinforcement, you must dish out for a greater iCloud plan. This is too essential even to consider skipping. Just ensure that you back up on your iPhone.

2.2 Using Quick Start to Transfer Data to iPhone 11 Pro Max

With the "Quick Start" option, you can rapidly set up another iOS gadget using data from your current device. You can re-establish the remainder of your information and substance to your new gadget from your iCloud backup. In case you are setting up another iPhone using your current iPhone—and the two devices are using iOS 12.4 or later—Quick Start offers the alternative of using iPhone relocation. This permits you to move every one of your information remotely from your current iPhone to your new one. Follow the instructions:

- To use "Quick Start", start your iPhone 11 Pro Max, and place it near to your new gadget that is also using iOS 12.4 or later.
- Quick Start gives the choice of using your Apple ID for setting up your new device. Make sure that it is the same Apple ID that you want to use. Tap "Continue". If you do not see anything to proceed, make sure that Bluetooth is turned on.
- Wait for a movement on the new gadget. Place your previous phone over the new phone. If you cannot use your previous device's camera, tap and you can "Authenticate Manually", then follow the on-screen instructions.
- Enter your previous device's password on your new gadget.
- Follow the directions to have a Face ID on a new gadget.
- Enter your Apple ID password on the new phone.
- Your new iPhone offers you to re-establish applications, and settings from your iCloud backup, or refreshing your previous device's backup and afterward re-establishing.
- After selecting a backup, you can choose to move a few settings related to area, Apple Pay, protection, and Siri.

2.3 Transfer Data Directly to Your iPhone 11 Pro Max

If both iPhones are using iOS 12.4 or later, the data transfer directly from one gadget to another is easy. Keep your previous iPhone near to your new one to keep the two iPhones associated with power. Get a Lightning to USB Cable and Lightning to USB 3 Camera Adapter. Follow these steps to complete the process:

- Attach the Lightning port to USB 3 Camera Adapter to control through its Lightning port.
- Make a point to use a 12W or higher force connector.
- Connect the Adapter to iPhone.
- Fit the Cable into your iPhone 11 Pro Max, then attach the other end to the connector.
- Complete the process by transferring files you want to transfer.

2.4 Activation of Apple ID

You need an Apple ID account to access all Apple services like music, App Store, iMessage, FaceTime, etc. and make the most out of your device.

You can do online shopping with this account from apple.com. If you already have an Apple ID, you do not need to make a new one. You can sign in with the existing one. When you sign in to the App Store and other services apps, you may need to include a credit card or other installment data. You cannot sign in to the App Store and other media administrations with more than one Apple ID simultaneously, or update the substance you purchase with an alternate Apple ID. Contingent upon how you made your Apple ID, you may be incited to move up to two-factor confirmation on a qualified gadget.

When you turn on your iPhone 11 Pro Max and try to set up your iPhone, you will find a notification that will require you to sign in with Apple ID. After signing in, all of the Apple services on the device will automatically be set up. If you are not sure about your Apple ID, try to search it by entering your full name and email address associated with your Apple ID. To handle your Apple ID, update phone numbers and devices, or manage a payment method, you can use the Settings App on iPhone 11 Pro Max.

Follow the steps given below to activate your Apple ID. Keep in mind that you need to have access to the internet to activate your account.

- o Go to "Settings"

- ○ Tap "Sign in to your iPhone."
- ○ If you do not have an Apple ID, tap "Don't have an Apple ID." Then, follow the on-screen instructions
- ○ Tap the space next to "Apple ID" and fill in the username that you want for your Apple ID.
- ○ Tap "Next"
- ○ Tap the area next to "Password" and type the password for your Apple ID.
- ○ Tap "Next"
- ○ Go back to the home screen

2.5 iCloud Setup

iCloud is the name Apple provides for its scope of cloud-based administrations, covering regions as various as contacts, email, calendar syncing, finding lost gadgets, and the iTunes Match. The purpose of cloud services, by and large, and iCloud, specifically, is storing data on a remote cloud server.

This implies that you are not occupying extra space on a specific gadget, and implies that you can get to the data from any web associated gadget.

iCloud lets you store data on the internet, and afterward get to this data from the entirety of your devices - iPad, iPhone, Mac, Apple TV, even Windows PCs.

However, if you visit iCloud.com and sign in to your record, you can see this straightforward idea's wide scope of apps. Here are some features of iCloud:

Contacts: If you give authorization, iCloud will match up Contacts over your iOS and macOS gadgets. This implies that you have to keep up just one rundown of contacts because any progressions you make on your iPhone will apply to Contacts on your Mac and different gadgets.

iCloud Drive: A straightforward method of putting away documents in the cloud.

Calendar: Likewise, iCloud synchronizes occasions over the entirety of your gadgets.

iWork: You can utilize Numbers, Pages, and Keynote as web apps, because of iCloud.

Notes: You can decide to spare Notes locally, yet matching up against them across gadgets is splendidly advantageous. This is how we plan notes for webcasts: type them into Notes on Mac, at that point, bring an iPhone onto the studio, and read them off.

Follow the instructions given below to set up iCloud:

- o On your iPhone 11 Pro Max, go to "Settings"
- o Tap "General"
- o Choose "Software Update". Check whether there is an update accessible.
- o Go to "Settings" again and sign in to your gadget with your Apple ID.
- o At the point when you sign in, iCloud starts to work automatically.
- o To check your iCloud settings:
- o Go to "Settings" on the home screen.
- o Tap [your name], then select "iCloud".
- o Pick the apps—like "Calendars", "Contacts", and any other app—that you need to use with iCloud.
- o Set up "iCloud" on your other gadgets to keep your data up-to-date.

2.6 Setting Date and Time

It is crucial to set the date and time correctly, as some iPhone functions would not work otherwise. To set date and time, follow the instructions:

- o Go to ""Settings"
- o Tap "General"
- o Tap "Date & Time"

o   Turn on automatic updating of time zone, date, and time by tapping the "Set Automatically" button.

o   Go back to the home screen. It is done.

2.7 Connect iPhone 11 Pro Max to Computer

You can quickly transfer files, such as audio files or photos between your phone and computer. Follow the instructions given below:

o   Connect the data cable to your computer's USB port and the socket.

o   Before you try to connect your computer and phone, you will need to install iTunes on computer.

o   Go to "iTunes"

o   You will be able to transfer files as soon as you add your files to the iTunes library.

o   Tap "Add File to Library". You will have to add one file at a time.

o   To add a folder, tap "Add Folder to Library".

o   Go to the "file" or "folder" in the computer's file system. Then simply follow the on-screen instructions to add a folder or file to your iTunes library.

o   The transfer will start automatically if the setup has been done or you can manually begin to transfer by clicking the iPhone icon.

o   Tap the required category, then follow the on-screen instructions for required settings.

o   Tap "Apply".

o   Transfer Images and Videos from iPhone 11 Pro Max to your computer

o   Go to the "File Manager" on your computer.

o   Go to the folder you want to transfer to your iPhone's file system.

o   Highlight the file or folder.

o   Copy or move it to the location where you want the transfer.

2.8 Bluetooth Devices

Bluetooth is a wireless connection. It is helpful when you have to connect to other nearby devices. For Bluetooth device setting, follow the given instructions:

o   Tap "Settings" from the home page of your iPhone.

o   Go to "Bluetooth"

o   Tap the indicator near to the "Bluetooth" button to turn on the function.

o   To pair Bluetooth devices with your iPhone, tap that Bluetooth device, and follow the on-screen instructions to pair that device with your iPhone.

o Ensure that the Bluetooth device is turned on and ready to connect.

2.9 Use of Face ID

The function of Face ID is to use facial recognition to unlock your iPhone 11 Pro Max. It confirms your identity in apps. In some cases, facial recognition will not work, so you must set up a PIN. You can have authenticated purchases in Apple Pay, iTunes Store, Book Store, App Store, and Books App with your Face ID. To set up Face ID, follow the instructions given below:

o Tap "Settings" from your iPhone home page.

o Go to "Face ID & Passcode"

o Click "Set up Face ID"

o Hold your iPhone so that it is at your eye level, then tap "Get Started"

o Place your face position in the circle and rotate your head.

o When the scan is done, tap "Continue".

o Repeat this step to scan your face one more time.

o Click "Done"

o You need to enter a passcode in case Face ID cannot be used, or not available at that time.

o Confirm passcode by re-entering it.
o Put the password of your Apple ID.
o Tap "Continue"
o To unlock your iPhone with Face ID, look at your iPhone, and swipe up at the same time from the bottom of the screen.
o Unlock it.

2.10 Use of Dark Mode

Dark Mode alternative gives the whole iOS experience a wonderful dim shading effect that is ideal for low-light conditions. When Dark Mode is on, the light from the gadget will not upset the individuals around you. Having a dim mode on gadgets just like iPhone 11 Pro Max could enhance how you take a gander at the things in your gadget. Even though it probably would not seem a significant issue for other people, having a dim mode could likewise give other extraordinary advantages. It permits you to spare battery utilization on your gadget.

Enacting dim mode could likewise reduce eye exhaustion while utilizing iPhone 11 Po Max for an all-inclusive period. If you are encountering affectability to phone lights, at that point, you can utilize your cell phone. You should not have to stress over any symptoms with the assistance of dark mode. Here is how to utilize dark mode settings on iPhone:

- Go to "Settings".
- Click "Display & Brightness".
- Click on "Automatic mode" to activate.
- Click on "Dark" if not to activate it manually.
- Tap "Options".
- Click "Custom Schedule".
- Tap "Light Appearance".
- Choose preferred time to flip to light mode.
- Then go to "Dark Appearance."
- Select your preferred time to switch to Dark mode.

Activation of the dark mode is simple and easy. Keep exploring new features and educate yourself with the various options on iPhone 11 Pro Max. There is a lot more for you.

2.11 Security and Privacy

Here are some settings you should make, and changes you should make to solidify the security and lockdown your gadget, alongside a visit through a portion of the new security and protection highlights.

Set a Strong Passcode

No matter how much you feel secure to have Face ID to access an iPhone, having a secure passcode is still a better option.

- Tap on "Settings" from the home screen.
- Tap "Face ID & Passcode".
- Enter your password, and then click "Passcode Options" to have more options.
- Choose one option from the given options and make a secure passcode.

Block Unwanted and Unknown Callers

To use this feature and to get rid of spam calls, follow the given instructions:

- Tap on "Settings"
- Tap on "Phone"
- Switch to "Silence Unknown Callers"

Block Access of Apps to Bluetooth

In your iPhone 11 Pro Max having iOS 13, you may see apps asking you to transfer data with Bluetooth. You will have an option to accept or reject access, or you can tap on Settings. Tap on Privacy, and go to Bluetooth and do the required changes there.

Enable iOS Automatic Updates

iOS 13 can update automatically. This should always be like that. You can also check it by going to Settings. Tapping on "General", and then go to the "Software Update" and check "Automatic Updates" is working and enabled.

Control Location Sharing

In iPhone 11 Pro Max, you can get notifications telling you about apps that are using location data. It gives you the choice to keep it that way or block it.

- o   Go to "Settings"
- o   Tap on "Privacy"
- o   Go to "Location Services"
- o   Change permissions for apps.

Finding your iPhone

iPhone 11 Pro Max has a new cool app named "Find My" that you can use anytime to locate your family and friends, share your location, or find your lost device. This app has two amazing features. The first one is to "Enable Offline Finding", which tracks your lost device not connected to Bluetooth or Wi-Fi. The second one is "Send the Last Location" that sends your device's location to Apple whenever the battery is low.

Control the Accessibility of Items when your iPhone is Locked

Manage how much you want to have accessible when your device is locked. The more security you will have if you lock important things on your device. To do this:

- o   Tap on "Settings"
- o   Go to "Face ID & Passcode"

- o Enter your passcode.
- o Take control of the accessibility.

Minimize the Lock Screen Time

If there is less lock screen timeout, your iPhone or iPad can act faster to have authentication to unlock it.

- o Go to "Settings"
- o Tap on "Display & Brightness"
- o Choose "Auto-Lock"

Apart from having two-factor authentication, setting up a "Recovery Key" will also enhance security.

Control Access with Safari

Under iOS 13, in iPhone 11 Pro Max, the Safari browser can control access to features like the microphone, the camera, and the current location.

- o Tap on "Settings"
- o Go to "Safari"
- o Look for "Settings For Websites"

Setting up Two Factor Authentication

To secure your data, utilize two-factor authentication. Even when a hacker has your credentials on iCloud, Apple will immediately send a code, which will block attacks. Follow the instructions below:

- o Tap on "Settings"

- ○ Click on your name.
- ○ Tap on "Password & Security"
- ○ Select "Two-Factor Authentication"

2.12 Tips for Using IOS 13

iOS 13 is one of Apple's latest operating systems for iPads and iPhones. Apple introduced the latest iOS operating system i.e., iOS 13, on June 3, at the event of the Worldwide Developers Conference 2019. iOS 13 offers a long list of new and exciting features. Apple surpassed its expectations with its optimization trend by making iOS 13 more efficient and faster than ever. App updates have improved download sizes of apps have been reduced, app launch times are much quicker, and Face ID is much faster. There is a "Dark Mode" option available that enhances the entire outlook of the operating system.

Enjoy the Dark Mode

The dark mode in iOS 13 flips the whole color scheme, showing back background and pure white text. It also enhances battery life. To activate dark mode, go to "Control Center", then press and hold on "Brightness". You will find an "Appearance" button. Choose it to put your iPhone to the Dark mode. You can make a customized schedule based on any time in a day.

Safari Download Manager

Safari has a download manager on iOS 13. Whenever you try to reach a download link, you will see a pop-up having a "Download" tab on it. Press it, and you will find a "Download" tab right next to the URL section. From here, you can manage all downloads. Download files will automatically be saved in iCloud to a folder named "Downloads"

Volume HUD Screenshot in iOS 13

When you first tap on the "Volume" button, you can see a volume HUD right next to the volume buttons. The indicator shrinks by tapping the volume button again. But when it is in its thick form, you can press and drag on it to change the volume.

New Copy/Paste Gestures

iPhone 11 Pro Max has just made things easier for you, including text manipulation. You can now press and hold the cursor to move it all around with the utmost ease. To cut text, use a double three-finger pinch. To copy text, use a three-finger pinch, and to paste it, a three-finger expand is used.

Change File Download Location

In iOS 13, you can change the default download location. To do so:

- o Tap on "Settings"

- Go to "Safari"
- Go to "Downloads" and choose "On".
- You can always select any folder of your choice.

New Undo/Redo Gestures

To undo text entry, use three fingers, swipe left, and to redo, swipe right with three-finger.

Formatting Bar

To get a new formatting bar, if you do not like swiping, you can use the press and hold option using three fingers. In this way, you can Copy, Cut, Paste, Redo, and Undo.

New View of Photos App

The new "Photos" App comes with an "All Photos" section, having new places for various time periods. The most exciting part is the "Years" section.

New Feature in Photo Editor

iOS 13's new feature in Photo editor is simple and easy to use. You can edit the elements like vibrancy, brightness, saturation, the intensity of filters, and much more. It is simple to use and more efficient. In the Photos App, you also have the option to edit videos. You can apply new editing effects, rotate and crop the video, have a different aspect ratio, and much more.

Health App Menstrual Cycle Tracking

In iOS 13, there is a new menstrual cycle feature that is private in the Health App. It comes with reminders and tracking of periods and fertility.

New Gesture Typing

The one-handed typing has become much more comfortable with iOS, as you can type by just swiping your fingers on the keyboard.

Sharing an Entire Folder Using iCloud Drive

You can share folders from iCloud Drive to other users.

- o To do this, go to the "Files" App.
- o Press and hold on a particular folder, then select "Share"
- o Click "Add People"
- o You can use the "Mail" App or "iMessage"

Disable Bluetooth for Apps

Most of the apps, not all of them, turn on Bluetooth to track your current location. You have the option to block Bluetooth for any other app.

- o To do so, tap on "Privacy"
- o Go to "Bluetooth". Here you can see apps that ask for Bluetooth access.
- o Block access for apps that you want to block.

Set your Favorite Locations in Maps

Go to the "Maps" App and tap on the "Frequent Locations" tab. Tap on the "Add" button for location search. Then add a location.

Use Two AirPods on your iPhone

For you and your friend to enjoy the same things on iPhone with both having AirPods, just go to "AirPlay" in "Control Center" and allow the second "AirPods" to have a connection.

Use Find My App to Track Your Offline Apple Devices

In the new "Find My" app, there is a new feature of new offline device tracking. When the app is activated, go to "settings" and make sure it is enabled. You can track your lost offline Apple device.

iOS 13 Downloads Limit for Apps

The app's download limit of 200MB has been removed in iOS 13. While downloading a big app, you will be asked to make sure you want to go ahead. There is also an option to disable this prompt forever. To do so, go to "Settings", then the "iTunes & App Store". Choose "App Downloads".

Sharing ETA

You can now share an ETA. The person should be using "Messages" or "iMessage". It will make them enable to control your current location from the "Maps" App.

Drag Scrollbar for Quick Navigation

In iOS 13, the scrollbar can be dragged. Tap on it, and then move it quickly to go to any place on the page.

New Location of Shuffle and Repeat Tabs

The position of "Shuffle" and "Repeat tabs" has been changed again. Go to "Now Playing", press the "Up Next" button. You will find these tabs at the top.

Go to Open Safari from Search

If you cannot locate a particular tab, then type that tab name in the "Smart Search". Click "Enter". Safari will automatically lead you to the open tab instead of loading and searching the page again.

Set iMessage Custom Profile

In iOS 13, a new feature sets a customized iMessage profile with a photo and a name. You can also choose whom to share with.

- o Tap "Settings"
- o Go to "Messages"
- o Tap "Share Name and Photo"

- ○ Select from given options to share it with someone.

Close Tabs Automaticall

There is a new feature to close Safari tabs that you are not using automatically. You can have this option while trying to shut down all tabs at a time, or you can also do this manually. To do so, tap on "Settings", then go to "Safari". Choose "Close Tabs".

Connect External Storage

You can now connect a Card Reader or a USB drive to your iPhone by using a cable to access files in the "Files" App.

Scan Documents

Tap the "Files" App and go to the "Menu" button to see the "Scan Documents" option. It is a new feature. It works exactly the way as the "Notes" App does.

Optimize Battery Life

There is a new feature named "Optimized Battery Charging". It helps in optimizing battery life. The iPhone tracks your charging routine.

New Updates Option in the App Store

The "Updates" tab has been put to a new place in iOS 13. You will see the "Arcade" tab in place of the "Updates" option.

To find the Updates, tap on "Today", then go to the Profile icon. Here you can find the Updates section. To delete an app from your iPhone, just swipe towards the left side.

Use New Features in Mail App

In iOS 13, the "Mail" App has a new feature of formatting options. Press the box and then press Left Arrow. In this way, you can create a new toolbar. Press the "Aa" to see the new formatting feature. You can also change the font size, font, font style, and much more here.

Add Shortcuts Automation

In iOS 13, "Shortcuts App" supports Automation. With this feature, the creation of shortcuts has become easy. Go to the "Shortcuts" App and find the new "Automation" tab. Press the Plus button. You are ready to get started.

Create Multiple Bookmarks

In Safari in iOS 13, there is a new feature to save and open multiple tabs as bookmarks quickly. Press and hold Bookmarks, go to "Add Bookmarks" option. All tabs are saved as bookmarks in a single folder. You can open all of them at once.

New Zip/Unzip Feature for Files

In the Files app, press and hold a zip file. Uncompress option will show up to unzip that file.

You can compress a folder or even multiple files like this.

Full Page Screenshots

Take a screenshot and press preview in Safari. A new "Full Page" option will be shown. Press it. You will get the entire page screenshot.

Organize Files

You can now customize the "Local Storage". Go to the "Files" App. You can make multiple folders. You can even move files without using iCloud Drive.

For Wi-Fi Networks, Utilize Low Data Mode

On the info page of a Wi-Fi network, there is a new feature called "Low Data mode". Put it on, and enjoy this feature for specific networks.

Save Screenshots Directly to Files App

While saving a new screenshot, an option named "Save to Files" will pop-up. By using it, a screenshot can be saved directly in a folder in the Files App.

Updates and Customization

Always remember to make sure that the apps are updated. iOS 13 gives you a lot in its updated apps.

Take time to check for new updates and fully explore their updated features. Tap on "Settings". Go to the "Control Center", and find out what new features and options are available.

Chapter 3: Using Siri on iPhone 11 Pro Max

In this chapter, we will see what Siri is and what it can offer to you. This chapter will teach you to choose Siri settings on your iPhone 11 Pro Max. You will also learn how to use Siri and tell Siri about yourself to make the most out of this fantastic function.

3.1 Siri at a Glance

Siri works just like your personal assistant. Siri's Watch Face serves up suggestions, news and events. Siri can also search and send a book. It is incredible how quickly it finds photos, locates your car, unearths what you are looking for in the files, and gets you a ride. Siri is learning all the time to be more helpful. Learning is making Siri even smarter. You can always personalize Siri for more useful things. Just tell Siri about family members, and say some unusual words to make it recognizable for future use. Siri protects your private information. It is programmed to do a lot of learning while being offline. Searches are not related to your identity. To turn Siri hands-free on, you just need to say"Hey Siri." You can also just press a button. It will then always be there for help. SiriKit will let Siri function with all other apps.

Siri does a lot more for you without asking. Siri holds a connection without even lifting your finger. It can also send texts or make calls for you if your hands are busy, or you are driving. It can announce your incoming messages on AirPods. It offers suggestions like messaging someone that you will be late for lunch. Siri sets a reminder for you to make important calls like "Hey Siri, make a call to Dad on speaker." It announces your messages on AirPods like "Text Michael 'I'm on my way," "Message Alex 'I will be there in 10 minutes."Siri can also help you if you want to know who is calling you. Siri can finish your sentences.

It is a much easier and faster way to complete all sorts of important things. Setting timers, alarms, reminders, getting directions, and previewing your calendar, Siri can tell what you want to help you go through the day. With Siri Shortcuts, you have a faster way to access your apps. Siri will let you know the time to leave while analyzing traffic. By creating shortcuts from apps for the things you often do like, "Hey Siri, make a reminder for 15 minutes." Siri also suggests various shortcuts that are based on a daily routine. Siri Shortcuts will let you interact with other apps, just like having a conversation.

Siri can always find your favorite song. All you have to do is to ask Siri. Siri can suggest your favorite playlist whenever you start driving to go back home. Just click on play. You can ask Siri, "What music is this?" Siri is also a fantastic way to manage your home. You can manage your appliances and check their condition by just using your voice. Siri recognizes family members' voices by learning about it. Siri has solutions and answers to all sorts of questions.

3.2 How to Use Siri

You can easily control most of your phone's features with your voice. You can also call contacts from your address book, write messages, and internet surfing. Before you use voice control, you have to set up your phone for an internet connection and then turn on Siri. Here is how to do that:

- o Tap and hold the Side button of the phone.
- o If you already have turned on automatic activation, the voice control activation can be done by just saying, "Hey Siri."
- o Say in your own words that you would like the iPhone to do for you.
- o If any app is open on the phone, you can use this available feature.
- o You can say "Help" for more searches.

o Go back to the home screen.

3.3 Choosing Siri Settings

Follow these steps to choose Siri settings:

o Go to "Settings."
o Go to "Siri & Search."
o Select the indicator right next to "Press Side Button for Siri".
o Press "Enable Siri."
o Select the indicator right next to "Listen for "Hey Siri". If you turn this feature on, you need to follow the on-screen instructions to set up Siri. So it can recognize your voice.
o Select the indicator right next to "Allow Siri When Locked" to set it on or off.
o To use Siri, turn "On" the use of the phone lock code.
o Select "Language."
o Choose the language.
o Select the arrow left.
o Select "Siri Voice."
o Choose the accent.
o Select gender.
o Press the arrow left.
o Select "Voice Feedback."
o Select the required setting.
o Choose the arrow left.
o Select "My Information."

o   Select the required contact.

While choosing yourself as owner of your iPhone, your phone uses the information for various voice control features to navigate to the home address.

3.4 Get Yourself Introduced to Siri

By telling Siri about yourself, you can enjoy many personalized services. To tell Siri about yourself:

o   Go to the info card in the "Contacts" App.
o   Select "Settings."
o   Select "General."
o   Choose "Siri."
o   Go to "My Info", then select your name.
o   Include work and home addresses, and also your relationships.

Location information cannot be stored outside your iPhone. If you have no plan to use "Location Services" then:

o   Go to "Settings"
o   Choose "Privacy"
o   Select "Location Services" and turn it off.
o   Now Siri cannot do something that requires location information.
o   Once Siri identifies who you are, it can automatically set up reminders at the

addresses associated with your entrance in the "Contacts App."

Adding additional details about a particular contact will help Siri identify even more about you. Go to "Siri" and say a contact's name, then its relationship with you – for example, "Alicia Williams is my sister." Siri will ask you to confirm if the relationship is right. You can also say, "Call Dad" or "email Girlfriend," it will automatically know whom to contact. A lot of other things can also be added relating to your work or your favorite places etc.

Chapter 4: Messages and Email Settings on iPhone 11 Pro Max

In this chapter, we will learn Messages and Email settings in your iPhone 11 Pro Max. With the new iOS in iPhone 11 Pro Max, you can enjoy many new and amazing features in SMS, MMS, iMessaging, and Email to view and share your images and videos to another person and on social media.

4.1 SMS Settings

SMS is the text message that you can send to other phone users. You can send and receive messages without any setting in any complicated settings. You just need to insert your SIM. Then you are ready to go. If it does not happen, you can always set up iPhone 11 Pro Max for text messages manually. Follow these steps:

○ Go to your iPhone's home screen.
○ Select the message sign at the bottom of the screen.
○ Choose "Continue."
○ Select the option "Set up Later in Messages."
○ Select the compose sign.

o   You need to enter your number here, so tap on the plus sign.
o   Select any contact.
o   Select "Text Message."
o   Type a message.
o   Select the send sign.
o   It is done
o   Go back to the home screen.

Block Unwanted Incoming Messages

It is essential to know that you cannot block anonymous text messages. To block unwanted messages from the contact saved in your phone, follow these steps:

o   Go to your iPhone's start screen.
o   Select the phone sign.
o   Select "Recents."
o   Select the information sign.
o   Tap on "Block this Caller."
o   Tap on "Block Contact."
o   The contact has successfully been added to blocked callers.
o   Go back to the start screen.

4.2 MMS Settings

An MMS is a form of message that contains pictures and other files. It can then be sent to other iPhone users. You can immediately send and receive MMS messages after inserting your SIM in your iPhone 11 Pro Max. You can also set up your iPhone manually for MMS. Follow these steps:

- o Go to your phone's start screen.
- o Select "Settings."
- o Select "Mobile Data."
- o Tap on "Mobile Data Network." Without it, you cannot do manual configuration.
- o Go back to the start screen.

To complete this process, you need to restart the phone for the activation of this feature. Your iPhone 11 Pro Max will then automatically be configured for using MMS. To restart your phone, follow these steps:

- o Tap and hold the Power Tab and the Volume Up Tab, which you can find on the side of the phone.
- o Place the on/off sign to the right.
- o Your iPhone has been shut down.
- o To turn it on, tap and hold the power tab on the side of the phone.
- o Enter your PIN code.
- o Choose "OK."

o   The activation is complete when you send your first MMS. You can check the settings by sending MMS to one of your phone numbers if you do not want to send it to someone else.

o   If it has been sent, you will receive a confirmation message within a few minutes.

4.3 iMessaging Settings

You can only send iMessages to a contact number or an email address if the other person has a phone that supports iMessage. To make settings on your iPhone for iMessaging, it is necessary to activate Apple ID. Follow these steps:

o   Tap "Settings."
o   Tap "Messages."
o   Turn the "iMessage" feature on.
o   Press the tab right next to "iMessage." It will be turned on.
o   Tap on the indicator right next to "Send as SMS."
o   If this function is turned on, iMessages will be sent in the form of text messages when the service is not available.
o   Go back to the home screen.

4.4 Email Account Settings

One of the most fantastic apps in the iPhone 11 Pro Max is the "Mail" App. It is an email processing platform to get access to your emails, both personally and professionally, on the go. Using the "Mail" App is a lot easier now to ensure that all the users would not face a hard time.

You can start viewing, sharing, and responding to your emails as soon as you have an email account correctly set, and make sure that your iPhone has a stable network connection. To use email services, the user needs an account with a provider. You have different options regarding providers. Choose a provider to configure email on iPhone 11 Pro Max.

- Xtra Mail
- Gmail
- Spark Business Mail
- Yahoo
- Outlook.com

Xtra Mail

To activate Xtra Mail email on Apple iPhone 11 Pro Max, follow these steps:

- Go to the home screen.
- Select "Settings."

- Tap on "Passwords & Accounts."
- Tap on "Add Account."
- Select "Other."
- Tap on "Add Mail Account."
- Enter your name in the "Name" Tab, your "First" and "Last" name is enough.
- Enter the Xtra email address in the "Email" Tab.
- Enter the password in the "Password" Tab.
- Enter Xtra Mail in the "Description" Tab.
- Select "Next."
- Tap on "POP."
- Enter your name in the "Name" Tab, your "First and Last" name is enough.
- Enter Xtra Mail in the "Description" Tab.
- Put pop3.xtra.co.nz in the "Incoming Mail Server" Tab.
- Go to "Host Name."
- Add a full email address in the "Username" Tab.
- Add Xtra Mail password in the "Password" Tab.
- Go to "Outgoing Mail Server."
- Write "send.xtra.co.nz" in "Host Name" Tab.
- Select "Save."
- The information you put will be verified.
- If any error message appears, verify the settings again and tap on "Save."
- Select your email account.

- Select "SMTP" in "Outgoing Mail Server."
- Select "send.xtra.co.nz" in the "Primary Server tab."
- Turn on "Use SSL."
- Enter 465 in "Server Port."
- Select "Done."
- Select your email account.
- Go to "Advanced."
- Turn on "Use SSL."
- Enter 995 in "Server Port."
- Select your email account.
- Select "Done."
- Your email account has successfully been configured.
- Go back to the start screen.

SMTP verification is required for most email providers. After following the above instructions, if the service is not active, then disable SMTP verification, and try again.

Gmail

To activate Gmail email on Apple iPhone 11 Pro Max, follow these steps:

- Go to the home screen.
- Select "Settings."
- Tap on "Passwords & Accounts."
- Tap on "Add Account."
- Select "Google."
- Tap on "Continue."

- Go to "Email" and enter the email address.
- Tap on "Next."
- Select "Enter Your Password." Enter the password.
- Tap on "Next."
- Select "Save."
- Your email account has successfully been configured.
- Go back to the start screen.

Spark Business Mail

To activate Spark Business Mail email on Apple iPhone 11 Pro Max, follow these steps:

- ○ Go to the home screen.
- ○ Select "Settings."
- ○ Select "Passwords & Accounts."
- ○ Tap on "Add Account."
- ○ Select "Other."
- ○ Tap on "Add Mail Account."
- ○ Enter your name in the "Name" tab, your "First" and "Last "name is enough.
- ○ Enter the "Spark Business Mail" email address in the "Email" Tab.
- ○ Enter the password in the "Password Tab."
- ○ Enter "Spark Business Mail" in the Description Tab.
- ○ Tap on "Next."
- ○ Tap on "POP."
- ○ Enter your name in the "Name" Tab, your First and Last name is enough.
- ○ Enter the "Spark Business Mail" email address in the "Email" Tab.
- ○ Enter "Spark Business Mail" in the "Description" Tab.
- ○ Go to "Incoming Mail Server."
- ○ Type "pop3.sparkbusinessmail.co.nz" in "Host Name" tab.
- ○ Type your "Spark Business Mail" email address in the "Under Username" Tab.

- Type your "Spark Business Mail" password in the "Under Password" Tab.
- Go to "Outgoing Mail Server."
- Type "smtp.sparkbusinessmail.co.nz" in "Under Host Name" Tab.
- Type your "Spark Business Mail" email address in the "Under Username" Tab.
- Type your "Spark Business Mail" password in the "Under Password" Tab.
- Select "Save."
- The information you put will be verified.
- If any error message appears, verify the settings again and tap on "Save."
- Select your email account.
- Choose "SMTP" in "Outgoing Mail Server."
- Choose "smtp.sparkbusinessmail.co.nz" in "Primary Server."
- Turn on "Use SSL."
- Enter "587" in "Under Server Port."
- Choose "Done."
- Select your email account.
- Select "Advanced."
- Turn on "SSL."
- Enter "995" in "Under Server Port."
- Select your email account.
- The email account has successfully been configured.
- Return to the start screen.

SMTP verification is required for most email providers. After following the above instructions, if the service is not active, then disable SMTP verification, and try again.

Yahoo!

To use email on your iPhone 11 Pro Max, you need to create an account with Yahoo! Follow these steps to configure Yahoo! email on Apple iPhone 11 Pro Max.

- Go to the home screen.
- Tap on "Settings."
- Select "Passwords & Accounts."
- Tap on "Add Account."
- Tap on "YAHOO!"
- Select "Email" and enter the email address.
- Tap on "Password" and enter the password.
- Select "Save."
- The email account has successfully been configured.
- Return to the start screen.
- You can use this email to send and receive emails.

Outlook.com

Follow the instructions given below to know how to configure Outlook.com email on iPhone 11 Pro Max:

- o Go to the home screen.
- o Select "Settings."
- o Select "Passwords & Accounts."
- o Go to "Add Account."
- o Tap on "Outlook.com."
- o Select "Email," then enter the email address.
- o Tap on "Next."
- o Tap on "Password," then enter the password.
- o Tap on "Sign in."
- o Tap on "Save."
- o The email account has successfully been configured.
- o Go back to the home screen.
- o Your account is ready to send and receive the email.

Solving Mail App Troubleshooting Issues in iPhone 11 Pro Max

The following are some of the solutions to Mail app troubleshooting issues in the iPhone 11 Pro Max.

Sometimes after updating the latest iOS, you can face some problems, and your app might not work. These methods will help eliminate those factors that might have stopped the Mail app from working correctly on iPhone. Before going towards the solution, make sure there is a problem. For that login to your account, and check for new emails in the inbox.

If new emails do not show up on your iPhone, then there is a problem waiting to be solved. Let's learn how to solve it:

Restart the Mail App

The "Mail" App might get disturbed after the update. It might no longer be able to load up. This problem happens when you leave the "Mail" App running in the background while updating. Any app would have the same adverse effect when left suspended while updating. To solve this problem, close the Mail app, then restart your iPhone. Just follow these steps:

Swipe up on the screen, and then stop when you reach the middle of the screen. Pause until the app previews show up.

- o Swipe sideways to locate the Mail App preview.
- o Swipe up on the "Preview Card" to close the app.
- o You should also clear out all other apps on the background to prevent them from interfering with your Mail App. After closing all background apps, proceed with these steps to reboot your iPhone:
- o Tap and hold the "Side" and the "Volume Up" tabs for a couple of seconds.
- o Release these tabs when the "Slide to Power off" section appears.

- o Swipe the bar to turn the device off.
- o After a few seconds, tap and hold the "Side" Tab.
- o Release it when the Apple logo shows up.

Manage Restrictions in Mail App

Apps may be blocked by iPhone restrictions. When they are enabled, you might not be able to run certain apps. Follow these instructions to see and manage the restrictions for Mail app on iPhone 11 Pro Max:

- o Tap "Settings."
- o Choose "General."
- o Select "Content & Privacy Restrictions."
- o If required, enter the screen time passcode to continue.
- o Navigate to "Allowed Apps."
- o Check that the "Mail" App tab is enabled. If it is not the case, then switch the tab next to "Mail" to "ON."
- o After making changes, re-enter your passcode, if required, to confirm.
- o Restart iPhone.
- o Re-launch the "Mail" App to check if emails are there in your inbox.

Refreshing Internet Connection

Another possible cause of your iPhone is unable to get emails after the recent update because it has some internet connection issues.

If the most recent update has caused your phone's internet connection, it can become a little bit shaky. To solve this, you can refresh your internet connection. Turning "Wi-Fi" off and then on again. Here is how you can do it:

- o Select "Settings" from the home screen.
- o Choose "Wi-Fi."
- o Press the "Wi-Fi" button to "OFF," or you can also use "Airplane Mode" to disable your device's wireless functions, then re-enable them all at once.
- o Tap "Settings."
- o Choose "Airplane Mode."
- o Switch the "Airplane Mode" button to "ON." It will disable your phone's wireless radios and other functions like Bluetooth and Wi-Fi.
- o When "Airplane Mode" is on, reboot your iPhone to clear out the cache.
- o After reboot is complete, tap "Settings."
- o Open "Airplane Mode."
- o Switch the "Airplane Mode" button to "OFF."
- o Reconnect the iPhone to Wi-Fi.
- o Wait for it to come back online.

There is another option of forgetting a Wi-Fi network that you are already connected to, then re-adding it. To do that:

- o Go to "Settings"

- o Choose the "Wi-Fi" menu. Make sure the "Wi-Fi" button is "ON."
- o While navigating to the networks, find your Wi-Fi connection.
- o Select your Wi-Fi network, then tap the "i" icon right next to it.
- o Choose "Forget This Network."
- o Press "Delete Network" to confirm the action.
- o Delete other Wi-Fi networks that are no longer in use, so they cannot interfere with the Wi-Fi network that you are connected to.
- o Once Wi-Fi networks are deleted, switch "Wi-Fi" to "OFF."
- o Restart your iPhone.
- o Go back to "Settings."
- o Select the "Wi-Fi" menu, and then switch "Wi-Fi" to "ON" again.
- o Look for your Wi-Fi network in the list, once found, select it, then press "Connect."
- o Enter the password to connect to the network.

When your phone is connected, go to the browser, and open different pages and websites. If all websites are quickly loaded, your internet connection is properly working, and so should the online apps.

To see if the problem is solved with the Mail App, launch the app, and create an email message. If you get the email to your personal account, then it means the problem has been resolved.

Re-adding your Email Account to iPhone 11 Pro Max

If the latest update damages your present email credentials, there are chances that your last email session has been expired. So, you need to log out. At the same time, if the recent update ruined your email account, you would have to delete it first and then set up a new one. Here is how to do it:

- o Tap "Settings" from the home screen.
- o Choose "Passwords & Accounts."
- o Go to the "Accounts."
- o Tap to choose the email account you want to delete.
- o Press "Delete Account."
- o Confirm by pressing "Delete from My iPhone."

After the email has been deleted, continue with following steps to re-add the email account manually:

- o Tap "Settings" from the home screen.
- o Choose "Passwords & Accounts."
- o Go to the "Accounts."

- o Choose "Other" from the given list of email providers.
- o Tap "Add Mail Account."
- o Type necessary information such as name, password, email address, and a short description for the email account.
- o Press "Next" to continue.
- o When "Mail" has found your email settings, your account has been set up.
- o Press "Done" to complete your setup.
- o After setting up the email account on "Mail," restart iPhone to apply the recent changes that you made.
- o Then go check your "Mailbox" to check if new emails are there.

Reset All Settings

The recent update that you made may have caused some severe issues in your phone's system. You can fix it and reset all the settings to restore the default settings. Follow these steps:

- o Tap on "Settings" from the home screen.
- o Choose "General."
- o Tap on "Reset."
- o Select "Reset All Settings."
- o Enter passcode if required to continue.
- o Confirm your action by tapping the above option for resetting all settings on your device.

After the resetting is done, you might need to re-enable some necessary features, especially those that were disabled by default. Make sure that the time and date information on your phone is correct. Use the "Automatic Date and Time" feature to make sure that it has been set to correct date and time, and it is based on the time zone of your current location.

To deal with complex post-update issues that might have changed the Mail App system and caused it not to function correctly and stopped working, you can choose iTunes. Using iTunes, you can always restore and repair significant issues in the system by restoring the iPhone in recovery mode. These methods require a computer that is either Windows or a Mac with the latest version of iTunes software. The main demerit for these methods is that they might result in permanent loss of your relevant data.

But they can also offer a higher passivity of resolving the broken system, including those affected by the update bugs.

Try to back up all crucial files from iPhone 11 Pro Max to the computer. You can utilize any one of these methods for restoring your iPhone from an iOS backup, or you can downgrade iPhone while letting Apple resolve issues for Mail.

You can also just toggle to other alternative email options such as Spark, Gmail, Spike, Outlook, etc. For more recommendations and further assistance, you can report your problem to your iPhone carrier or Apple Support.

4.5 Share Photos, Videos, and Location Data

To share photos and videos with someone else, you can use apps like Mail App or Messages App. You can also use third-party apps like Messenger and WhatsApp. With these apps, the quality of images and video files depends on the app. Photos are sent in Messages in high-resolution. There are options to choose the file size in the Mail app. WhatsApp compresses the files a lot. To send photos and videos in full-resolution, the Messages and the Mail Apps are the preferred options. Here are some simple steps for all apps:

- o Go to the "Photos" app on the iPhone.
- o Tap on "Select."
- o Select the images you want to share.
- o Tap on the "Share" button. You will see a list of apps in the second row to share your images.
- o Tap on the "Messages," then "Mail," or the "WhatsApp" app.

- You can share the videos with the same process.

To send the images and videos via iMessage, follow these steps:

- Go to "Messages."
- Click on the "To:" section, search for iMessage contact.
- Tap the contact name on the list.
- More than one contact can also be added.
- You will find the images in the text field. Tap on the "Send" tab. Your photos will be sent to the contact you selected.
- To see if your photos have been sent, go to the conversation section in the Messages App.
- Click on the "Send" button.

To send images through the Mail app, follow these steps:

- Go to "Mail."
- The "Compose" screen appears. The photos are shown on it as attachments.
- Tap on the "To:" section.
- Type the email address you want to share photos with.
- To add multiple contacts, tap on the plus sign.
- Type a message and a subject if you like to.
- Press the "Send" button.

- Go to the "To:" section.
- Write the email address, then click the "Send" button.
- A notification shows up to ask you if you want to reduce the image size. It is always best to select "Actual Size," as it keeps the full resolution. You can choose other options too if you like to. You have a choice.
- The "Large" option is also suitable as it significantly cuts the file size, keeping the image quality intact at the same time.

How to Share Photos and Videos from the Messages App

To send images through Messages App, follow these steps:

- Go to the "New Message" Tab.
- Press the "Photos" Tab.
- Select the images and videos that you like to share.
- Add contacts in the "To:" section for creating a new message,
- Add a comment if you wish to.
- Select the "Send" button.

Sharing or Removing Location Data from Photos in iPhone 11 Pro Max

When you capture a photo from your iPhone, iOS automatically utilizes GPS to record the location shooting spot's location.

It is of enormous convenience because it permits you to catalog many images according to location. It helps in sorting out shoots and assists in keeping track of friends and family over time. Often, the location metadata of images are welcome. Other times, it is not. While sharing a photo with geolocation coordinates found in a its EXIF data, viewers can utilize the Photos app to determine the place at which the shot was taken. When posting your photos to any social media site, you would not want to post an image close to your home, without removing the information for protecting your privacy. But, you can leave it as it is if you have no problem sharing it with others.

Removing Location Data

With iOS 13, Apple has enhanced its commitment to anti-tracking technologies and security issues by providing different ways to remove location information from images before sharing them with someone.

You can easily remove the location metadata from videos, photos, or multiple photos you want to send through any app.

In that way, there is no need to worry about a stranger finding out location from personal shots. Follow these steps to find out how to do it:

Find the video or image you like to share in your albums.

- o Tap the "Share" Tab.
- o To share multiple images or videos, click "Select" in the section view or the album.
- o Select all the files you want to send.
- o Press the "Share" Tab.
- o See a new "Options" Tab while sharing in the Photos App.
- o Send your image via any medium you like. There is no way for the viewer to find out the location where it was actually shot.

You can remove the location metadata within the iPhone 11 Pro Max Photos App, so be sure that you share your images directly from this app. This privacy feature has been designed only for the photos and videos you share with someone else. The images on your device will retain all their location data. It will only remove the data for the ones that you send via email, text, or any social media.

The rest of the metadata related to your images like Device Type, Time, Aperture, and Shutter Speed remains with your image.

You can know that location data was removed on your phone. To view where an image or video was taken, just swipe up in the Photos App.

The location must have been enabled when you had shot it, a map shows up pinpointing it in the "Places" section. In short, turning off your Location data using this new feature means that when you share any of your image or video, it will not carry the location data with it.

Chapter 5: Call Settings on iPhone 11 Pro Max

This chapter will discuss various features and settings of iPhone 11 Pro Max regarding Calls and Contacts, Caller ID and Call Forwarding, Setting Ringtones, Using FaceTime, and fixing some issues that you might face if you are unable to use call features properly in your iPhone 11 Pro Max

5.1 Managing Contacts

Let's learn exciting features that you can use to manage your calls and contacts in your iPhone 11 Pro Max.

Importing contacts to iPhone 11 Pro Max from Sim Card

Importing contacts from your Sim Card will save a lot of time. Let's learn the step by step guide to import your contacts

- o Go to the "Settings" Tab.
- o Choose "Contacts."
- o Tap on "Import SIM Contacts."
- o It will start transferring your SIM card numbers to the phone storage.

Create a New Contact on iPhone 11 Pro Max

You can always save your contacts in the address book of your phone. You can also save additional information such as personal ring tone and email address. To create a contact, follow the guidelines:

- ○ Go to "Contacts."
- ○ Tap on the "New Contact" icon.
- ○ Write down the name.
- ○ Tap on "First Name" and type the first name.
- ○ Tap on "Last Name" and type the last name.
- ○ Tap on "Add Phone."
- ○ Go to "Phone" and write down the phone number.

Follow the given instructions to add additional information such as a personal ring tone and an email address.

- ○ Press "Done."
- ○ Go back to the home screen.
- ○ Swipe up your finger on the screen to go back to the home screen.

Making a Call

You can make a call by finding and going to the contact number in the address book of your phone. To call a contact, follow these steps.

- o Press "Contacts."
- o Tap on the number you want to make a call to.
- o Ending a Call
- o Tap on the "End Call" icon to end the call.
- o Go back to the home screen.
- o Swipe up your finger on the screen to go back to the home screen.

Blocking Unwanted Calls

Keep in mind that the anonymous text messages and calls cannot be blocked. To block a contact, follow these guidelines:

- o Tap" Settings." from the home screen.
- o Go to "Phone."
- o Tap "Blocked Contacts.'
- o Go to "Add New."
- o Choose the contact that you like to block.

Contacts Back Up through iCloud

To back up your contacts through iCloud, follow these instructions:

- o Select the "Settings" App from the home screen.
- o Select "Passwords & Accounts"
- o Go to "iCloud."
- o Tap on "Contacts Switch."
- o Your job is done.

5.2 Caller ID and Call Forwarding

You can quickly turn On and Off your caller identification. Your contact number will not be shown to the other person while making a call if you have turned it off. But keep in mind that your number will only be hidden while making voice calls, not while sending messages.

- Press "Settings."
- Go to "Phone."
- Tap on "Show My Caller ID."
- Tap on the indicator right next to "Show My Caller ID." Turn the function "ON" or "OFF."
- Go back to the home screen. Swipe up your finger on the screen to go back to the home screen.

Turning on Call Forwarding Feature

To turn on the call forwarding feature, follow these steps:

- Select "Settings" from the home screen.
- Select "Phone."
- Select "Call Forwarding."
- Select the "Call Forwarding" switch to activate it. You have to be in the range of the cellular network to set your iPhone to forward calls.
- Press "Forward To." Enter the forwarding number you want to add.

- When you are finished with it, select "Back" to go back to the "Call Forwarding" screen.
- When the "Call Forwarding" feature is working and active, the "Call Forwarding Icon" appears in the "Control Center Status" bar.
- To turn this feature off.
- Go to the "Call Forwarding" screen, and tap the "Call Forwarding" switch to turn it"On".

5.3 Setting Ringtones

You can easily add a picture and a ringtone to any contact to make it more appealing and easy for you to manage.

Adding Photo and Ringtone to your Contacts

To add a photo, select "Add Photo" then locate the desired picture. For a ringtone, go to the "Ringtone" Tab. Choose the desired ringtone from the list, then tap on "Done." Select "Done" one more time to save the changes made to contact.

5.4 Phone Calls Settings

Here are some fantastic Phone Call settings that you can enjoy on your iPhone 11 Pro Max.

Turning Call Waiting "On" or "Off

When the call waiting feature is turned on, you can always answer a new incoming call without ending the ongoing call. To do the setting, follow these steps

- Press "Settings."
- Go to "Phone."
- Tap "'Call Waiting."
- Turn the indicator next to "Call Waiting" to "On" or "Off."
- Go back to the home screen.
- Swipe up the finger on the screen to go back to the home screen.

Turning Call Announcement "On" or "Off"

What a cool thing to have your phone saying the contact that is calling you. To turn on this feature for your phone to call out the contact name, you have to save the contact in the address book of your phone. Follow these guidelines

- Press "Settings."
- Go to "Phone."
- Tap on "Announce Calls."
- Select "Always" to turn on the feature in case the silent mode is turned off.
- Go to "Headphones & Car" to turn on the feature when the iPhone is connected to a car or a headset.

- Tap on "Headphones Only" to turn on the feature when the iPhone is just connected to a headset.
- Tap on "Never" to turn off this feature.
- Go back to the home screen.
- Swipe up your finger on the screen to go back to the home screen.

5.5 Using FaceTime

FaceTime requires a data plan, and the call recipient should also have a FaceTime-activated iOS phone. FaceTime with new features now supports up to 32 persons at one time. To activate FaceTime, follow these guidelines:

- Choose "Settings" from the home screen.
- Tap on "FaceTime."
- Select the "FaceTime" switch, and turn it on.

Making a FaceTime call with the help of the Phone App

To make a FaceTime call using the Phone app, follow the guidelines:

- Select the "Phone" App.
- Choose the "Contacts" Tab, then choose the desired contact.
- Make a FaceTime audio or video call, tap on the "Video" Tab, or the phone icon right next to FaceTime.

Making a FaceTime call with the help of the FaceTime App

- Select the "FaceTime" App from the home screen.
- Tap on a contact from the call history, or you can choose the "Add" icon for a new call.
- To answer an incoming FaceTime call, select an option.
- Choose "Accept" to accept it.
- Choose "Decline" to decline it.
- Tap on the "Message" icon, and then select the message, or you can select "Custom" to make and send a custom message.
-

You can also make a FaceTime call by using Dual SIM. Go to the "FaceTime" App, then select "Add." Choose the "Primary" or "Secondary" option. Then you are ready for a call.

5.6 Fixing Call Problems on iPhone 11 Pro Max

Make sure your iPhone has a stable cellular network connection. If the connection is not stable or weak, call and text features may not work on your phone.

Software-related problems that are affecting the iPhone's calling features are usually handled by carrying out some work. For as long as the iPhone is free from any kind of hardware damage, the chance of resolving the problem is definitely higher. Just give each solution a try.

Reboot iPhone 11 Pro Max

Restarting the phone can help fix many software issues, including the random call failures. Your saved data on the internal memory will not be affected. To back up files is not necessary. Follow these simple steps to soft reset or reboot iPhone 11 Pro Max:

- o Tap and hold the "Volume Up" and "Side" Tabs for a few seconds.
- o Let go of both buttons as soon as the "Slide to Power off" bar shows off.
- o Swipe it to turn the phone off.
- o After a few seconds, tap and hold the "Side" button. Release it when the "Apple" logo
- o Wait for the iPhone to complete rebooting. Allow it to re-establish network signals. As soon as the signal is ready, open the "Dialer" App, and then try a test call to ensure if it is working.

Switch the "Airplane Mode" On and Off.

Issues affecting the wireless features of the iPhone can also be solved by another simple feature called the "Airplane Mode" switch. It works by deactivating the wireless radios of the phone, including Bluetooth, Wi-Fi, and cellular data at the same time. Here is how you can do it:

- o Go to "Settings."
- o Choose "Airplane Mode."
- o Toggle the indicator right next to "Airplane Mode" to turn this feature on. All wireless features of your iPhone will be disabled simultaneously.
- o When the Airplane Mode is on, do a soft reset on your iPhone.
- o Wait until the phone is done rebooting. Then go to "Settings."
- o Go to the "Airplane Mode" menu.
- o Tap the "Airplane Mode" Tab again to disable the function.
- o When your phone has re-established the cellular network connection, try to place a test call to make sure it is working fine.

Install the Latest iOS

Install the latest iOS version that is available for iPhone 11 Pro Max. It can also help solve the problem if system bugs are causing it.

iOS updates also fix some patches to address widespread issues among iOS devices. Follow the steps to look for new iOS updates:

- o Tap "Settings."
- o Go to "General."
- o Click "Software Update."
- o A notification will appear if a new update is there. Follow the instructions to download, then install the update on your phone. It is advisable to have back up all important files before going for installation.

Reboot Network Settings

If there are any incorrect network settings or any kind of invalid network configurations that have been causing problems, this problem can be resolved by resetting the network settings on your iPhone. It will erase all current network settings, including Bluetooth connections, Wi-Fi networks, and Cellular settings. The errors will be removed. To know how to do this, follow these steps:

- o Tap on "Settings."
- o Choose "General."
- o Tap on "Reset."
- o Go to "Reset Network Settings."
- o Enter your password if required to continue.

- Tap on "Reset Network Settings" one more time to confirm the action.

When the reboot is finished, your iPhone will automatically restart. You just have to re-enable cellular data, Wi-Fi, Bluetooth, and other network functions to use them again on your iPhone.

Reinstalling your SIM Card

To use Cellular service, you need a SIM card. This SIM card must be installed with the right plan your iPhone account has been subscribed to. Therefore it should come from your network provider. So, be sure first to turn off your phone completely. It is a must-do for avoiding any kind of damage to your SIM card or the device itself. Proceed with these steps once the iPhone is shut down.

- Insert your SIM ejector into the hole on the tray situated on the right side of your phone.
- Push the SIM ejector till the tray pops out. Then pull the tray out.
- Now remove the SIM card.
- Carefully look at the card for any signs of damage like liquid traces or scratches.
- Place the card back into the tray. Make sure the gold contacts face down and the edge on the top right.

- o Push the card tray back into your phone till the point it fits into place.
- o Now you can turn the phone back on and retry making a call to ensure if it is working fine.

If you are not sure that the SIM card is the cause of the problem, insert it to your other device and see if you can do phone calls. If it is working on another device, then the SIM is not the cause. If it is not like that, then report the issue to your carrier and ask for a new SIM card.

Chapter 6: Camera Settings on iPhone 11 Pro Max

Camera is one of those features that are mostly used in the iPhone 11 Pro Max. Camera in the new iPhone 11 Pro Max is the most discussed app and feature. It is the first iPhone with a triple-camera to capture images up to a zoom level of 4x. It promises beautiful photos, even in a low light situation. It records high-quality videos. It means that the iPhone 11 Pro Max camera cannot be taken for granted. We all want bright and beautiful photos and videos daily. This chapter will discuss some cool features that the Camera in the iPhone 11 Pro Max has. We will also learn to view, share, and print your images and videos. In the end, we will have some solutions to troubleshooting problems regarding the use of Camera in the iPhone 11 Pro Max.

6.1 Taking Photos and Videos in iPhone 11 Pro Max

The iPhone 11 Pro Max has three stellar cameras that give you high zoom capabilities, a new feature called "Deep Fusion", and "Night Mode" options for capturing photos in dark places. It is not just the hardware alone that has been improved.

It is a new software that makes iPhone 11 Pro Max photos very sharp. Taking images with the latest iPhones is just as simple as it has always been on older models. Apple's new image features require more explanation, from a feature that helps to zoom out after taking the photo, to "Deep Fusion", and about the trade-off you first need to know before using it. Let's look at some of the fantastic tips and features that you should use in the Camera on your iPhone 11 Pro Max:

Quick Settings for Toggles

The next time you capture a group photo with an iPhone 11 Pro Max and make the best out of the built-in timer, there are chances that you may find it hard to find the toggle. Apple mostly moves the toggles in features like the filters and the timer, because they are not used that often. To place toggles where you can see them, press the arrow at the top of your phone screen if your iPhone's position is vertical. The arrow reveals the various toggles while changing the directions. You might see Live Photos, Flash, Aspect Ratio, Filters, and Timer. Hide them by pressing the button again once you are done. You can also swipe to view the toggles.

Zooming out Feature

iPhone 11 Pro Max models have an ultra-wide-angle camera. It is best to take pretty dramatic photos. Another cool feature in ultra-wide cameras is zooming out on an image captured with telephoto lenses or a wide lens. You can do this after taking the photo. It means if you took a group photo but just missed someone who could not get into the frame, you can always go back to the Photos app, and with the help of the crop tool, you can zoom out, which will bring that person back into the frame.

This is a very unusual feature. Your iPhone will always capture additional data around the spot of the video or an image you shoot. It gives you even more flexibility while editing the final video or picture. For video, it is turned on as standard. You need to go to "Settings", tap "Camera" to make settings for stills. To be able to see how it functions, activate this feature and try to take a shot at the normal focal length. View the photo in your "Camera" App, then tap "Edit". After that, find the size alteration tool. When you change the size, additional information of the shot appears, letting you much freedom to reframe the image completely.

To enable this feature, go to the "Settings" App and tap on "Camera". Go down and enable "Photo Capture Outside the Frame".

Anything captured outside of your image's frame will automatically be deleted, if not used, after 30 days. It depends on how the photo was taken. the iPhone may either recover the ultra-wide shot around the captured frame of the picture, it is when you can use a zoom out option, or it can capture two separate images and only show you the ultra-wide shot when you ask for it.

Quick Camera Settings

In iOS 13, Apple has pretty much cleaned up the Camera App interface. It has hidden a lot of settings that were used to be there on the screen. You can always find them by looking for an arrow icon on the screen with portrait orientation. Just press it, or just swipe through the viewfinder. It will reveal many icons below the viewfinder screen. You can always activate the "Live Motion" photos app, set the timer, alter the aspect ratio, or even add a filter. You can also see the Night Mode option when it is available.

Night Mode Feature

There is not so much to do for you when it comes to the Night Mode feature. Your iPhone automatically determines that there is not that much light available.

The Night Mode option will automatically show up right next to the arrow tab.

If its color is yellow, it means Night Mode is working. The tab will also show you the length of time, showing how long it will take to take the show. It indicates that after pressing the shutter, for how long you need to hold still. You can turn Night Mode off by only moving the slider upward or downward. You can have control over it. It is no lie that it is totally on the iPhone to control it. You can adjust the time duration to decrease or increase the amount of light captured by Night Mode.

Let's say you move the timer from 1s to 6s. Your iPhone 11 Pro Max will capture a brighter picture, which can lead to overexposure. On the other side, moving from 6s to 2s, the result can be a darker photo. Learn about different exposure by playing around these values. The fantastic thing about this feature is that it makes nighttime images look much brighter with more detailed quality.

Keep in mind that the Night Mode will not work as long as the light is right. It should not be selected every time. In low-light environments, when your iPhone can sense Night Mode, it will make a difference. It is shown in a Moon-Like tab when this feature is available for use in the upper left of the screen.

Deep Fusion

You do not need to turn on "Deep Fusion" toggle, iPhone 11 Pro Max will automatically capture photos with this new technology, but for that "Photo Capture Outside" the Frame should be turned off. If turned on, the iPhone will keep taking images that can be zoomed out later on, but "Deep Fusion" will not work. You also need to see that image capturing is being done with a 1x camera.

Fine-tuning of Zoom

When you are at a concert or want to capture your child in a school function, take advantage of all three cameras of your phone, and make the best out of their zoom levels. The iPhone 11 Pro Max has a wide camera, an ultra-wide-angle camera, and a telephoto camera. Each of these has 12 megapixels. It is interesting to learn that no matter which iPhone you use, the main Camera is always the wide Camera. It is labeled as "1x" in the app. To switch between these three cameras, you can press the zoom option. Your iPhone's viewfinder will automatically zoom in or zoom out.

To fine-tune the "Zoom" feature, scroll upward or downward to Zoom in or out in the iPhone 11 Pro Max new setup of the Camera.

You can also fine-tune how far to Zoom by pressing and holding on the Zoom level first, then drag the Zoom tool. If you select something apart from three fixed cameras, the photo quality suffers due to the digital zooming, despite using the focal lengths of these built-in cameras. These built-in cameras' focal lengths are fixed.

Changing Lenses

Go to the Camera App. Get yourself ready to explore the different lenses. To switch between these lenses, go to the bottom of your phone's viewfinder to see the tabs marked as 1x, 2x, and .5x. 1x is for a standard lens. By pressing 2, you will switch to the Telephoto Lens with a Zoom level of 2x. Press the .5x tab. You will switch to a wide-angle lens.

Try Slofie

A fantastic and fun feature on your iPhone 11 Pro Max is the Slofie App, which is a selfie that is a slow-motion video. It is not a still photo. It is straightforward to use, as you do not have to do much work. Your iPhone takes care of most of the tasks. Go to the Camera App. Choose Slo-mo from the given options. Switch the Camera to the front mode, then either press and hold the shutter button, or just single tap it.

If you chose to press and hold, you would see that the video stops recording as soon as you let go of it or press the tab to stop recording.

Your iPhone assembles this feature, so the first and ending part runs at the average speed, while the center of your video runs in slo-mo. The effect can be really dramatic, but you need to explore and try to get the best and desired results.

New Lighting Mode for Portrait

Go to the Camera App. Select Portrait mode on the section right above the shutter tab. Apple's Lighting Modes for portraits set a new trend in the market and remain some of the best available out there. In iOS 13 on the iPhone 11 Pro Max, you can try the different options available in the options list. There is an option that adds a white backdrop instead of a black backdrop after removing the subject's background. Like all other Portrait lighting modes, press the "Edit" Tab in the gallery. There you will see how the image looks with all different lighting options. Another fantastic feature in the Portrait mode is "Zoom Out". When you select this feature, the zoom level is, by default, at 2x. In the lower-left of the viewfinder, you can see the Zoom Tab, which, when pressed, reverts to the standard focal length. It gives you more freedom if the subject is close. You can also customize the lighting effect by pressing the hexagonal tab in the upper right of the screen.

Wide-angle Selfie

Fit your friends and the background into selfies with this fantastic feature. To use it, go to the Camera App, then switch to the Front Camera. Select "Photo mode". A small tab having two opposite-facing arrows should be at the top of the shutter button. Press this to have a wide-angle. You are ready to go.

Remarkable Video Camera

iPhone 11 Pro Max has lived up to its hype as a fantastic video camera. It has a long zoom range with a unique image stabilization option. This iPhone is definitely the best video camera in the market. It has a triple-camera lens. It records from video 4K to HD with a dynamic range and also the cinematic video stabilization function. Users can zoom anytime between each one of these three lenses. In iOS 13, many new editing tools for video permits users to crop, rotate, change exposure, and apply many amazing filters to videos. These settings are extremely easy to make. Smart HDR utilizes machine learning in order to identify subjects in your frame and then intelligently adjust them to look more natural with fantastic detail in it. In the "QuickTake" App, users can record a video by holding the shutter button.

6.2 View and Edit Photos and Videos

Apple has changed a lot the functioning of its editing software. It is even better in iOS 13. When you capture a shot that you would want to edit, later on, you just need to locate it in the "Camera Roll" App, then press the "Edit" Tab in the upper right of the screen. It has three main icons which you can find at the bottom of the screen. The first one is about adjusting the brightness, color, etc. the second one is for adding filters. The third one is for changing the aspect, ratio and size.

For each icon, settings can be made with the help of the tabs and sliders. To alter the size or shape of the photo, it is advisable to have it in a square rather than the 4:3 aspect ratio. You just need to press the aspect ratio tab in the upper right corner of the screen. Diffident sizes will be shown under the photo. On the tap of the screen, you will find tabs to mirror the picture or rotate it. When you are done with your editing, tap the "Done" Tab. Your photo will automatically be saved in the Camera Roll. In iOS 13, all these editing tools can be used on video too.

6.3 Fixing various Camera Problems in iPhone 11 Pro Max

You might face some troubleshooting issues while using Camera in your iPhone 11 Pro Max. Here are some of the best solutions to resolve these issues.

Update the Latest iOS Software

Update iPhone 11 Pro Max to the latest version available. It will help fix issues relating to Camera on iPhone. To check for updates to the newest version:

- o Tap "Settings"
- o Press "General"
- o Select "Software Update"
- o If the iPhone is updated, it will show that. If there is any available update, press "Download" and then press "Install" to begin the process.

Keep External Lens Clean

It may be one of the reasons that you have low-quality photos and videos. It might be because of the dirt on the external lens on your iPhone. Clean it with some lint-free cloth, and also the flash near your lens in a very circular motion with soft pressure. Do not clean it using fingers as this will damage and permanently scratch the lens.

Get Rid of Protective Casing

iPhone 11 Pro Max is a fantastic phone that you definitely love to protect. Try to keep it safe from any kind of physical damage. But here is the fact that some protective casing is an additional layer on the iPhone that may cause poor quality videos and photos. Apart from blurry images, you can also get dark images as some protective casing can affect the shot's whole lighting. To make sure if there is a difference, try to take a shot with and without your protective casing.

Choose the Right Type of Lens

iPhone 11 Pro Max has a triple-camera lens. It might be the reason for having camera issues of poor quality in your videos and photos. The reason is that you might not be using the right lens for a particular shot. To figure out which lens to utilize for a shot, check the capacity and limitations of each lens available on the iPhone 11 Pro Max:

Wide-Angle Lens: It is 25 mm. It works in the wide-angle range. It means that more areas can be included in one shot. This lens is best for architectural subjects and landscapes.

Telephoto lens: It is a 52mm lens. It works best to take pictures where your subject is far away from the camera. It can take a distortion-free and more detailed image.

It can also be used to take photos in Macro Photography and Portrait Mode.

Ultra-Wide-Angle Lens: It is a 3mm lens. It is used to take photos to cover more scenes. It has the same working as the Wide-angle lens, but it can capture the much wider landscape and architectural shots. It can also capture a photo of a particular scene that highlights your subject to make it look even larger than the background area of the shot.

It is noteworthy that iPhone 11 Pro Max has full capacity to make adjustments in the Digital Zoom. But still, it is advisable to use three lenses of iPhone 11 Pro Max rather than "Digital Zoom". The reason is that Digital Zoom can lead to undesirable results and poor quality of photos.

Close all of the Opened Apps and Restart your Camera App

There is also a possibility that you have been facing Camera issues because of running apps that may be causing your iPhone to function slower than usual.

Close opened apps and then restart the camera app to refresh iPhone 11 Pro Max. It can help in fixing Camera issues. Here is how you can close apps and restart your camera app:

- In order to close apps, swipe up the running apps and the Camera App.
- Restart the Camera App on your iPhone. You can search for it from your home screen.
- Press it to restart the Camera App.

Master Night Mode Settings

While taking a shot in the Night Mode setting, usually, it happens that a number that indicates the duration of time for that shot immediately appears. The timer can vary according to the lighting conditions of the shot. To avoid poor quality and blurry images, hold your iPhone still, or use a tripod, which is even a better option.

Clear Cache on iPhone 11 Pro Max

You might be experiencing some camera issues on the iPhone 11 Pro Max because of some apps that might be taking up space on the iPhone's processor. To fix this problem, you can clear the cache by following these steps:

- Tap on "Settings"
- Go to "General"
- Go to "iPhone Storage"
- You will see two options. One is "Offload Unused Apps", and the second one is to "Delete the App"
- Check all the apps and select the option you want for each app.

- o It will save the processor and storage space.

Restart your iPhone

Forceful restarting your iPhone 11 Pro Max might fix your camera issues. It refreshes the iPhone by forced closing of all unused running apps that are causing camera issues due to the delay in responding to the Camera App. Following steps will help you to restart your iPhone 11 Pro Max:

- o Tap and let go of the "Volume Up" Tab quickly. You can find that tab on the left side of your iPhone.
- o Tap and let go of the "Volume Down" Tab. You can find this tab on the left side right below the Volume up tab.
- o Tap and hold the "Sleep/Wake" Tab. On the right side of the iPhone 11 Pro Max, you can locate this tab.
- o When "Slide to Power Off" appears, release the "Sleep/Wake" Tab.
- o To shut down iPhone 11 Pro Max, swipe from the left to the right of the "Slide to power off" option.
- o Your iPhone 11 Pro Max will restart automatically.

Chapter 7: App Store on iPhone 11 Pro Max

This chapter will discuss one of the most used and fantastic features of the iPhone 11 Pro Max. We will go through different tabs available in the "App Store", serving different needs of the users. We will then learn to install and uninstall apps, along with some App Store settings, to benefit from the App Store functions fully.

7.1 App Store at a Glance

Apps have always transformed the way you like to do something; learning, creating, or playing games, and the App Store is the best place to search new apps that let you incredibly go towards your passions. App Store is one of the most crucial features of any Apple device. Through this medium, you can download, install new apps and other content. App Store is reliable as it is developed and maintained by the company itself. App Store Tabs make it easier to discover new and exciting apps. some of these tabs have been given below:

Today Tab

It is updated daily to keep you inspired and informed by the ever-changing world of games and apps.

It is also an exciting place to find other helpful tips and tricks of daily life.

Apps Tab

It is organized with recommendations to assist you in finding the right app for you. Keeping up with all the apps that mark their entry every week is a full-time task. Apple has a great team of editors who bring unique perspectives to the new world of apps.

Games Tab

Expert gamers manage it by taking your love for games to a whole new level.

Daily Stories

From world premieres to interviews, original news, and stories by the editorial team of Apple, this tab explores the effects of apps in this world of the digital era.

Lists

App Store team editors have developed lists of the most downloaded games and apps from finding the best apps for a healthy body to games. You can find all this in this tab.

Tips and Tricks

If you want to learn the use of filters in your Photo App in iPhone 11 Pro Max, this tab has got many "How-to" articles, tricks, and tips directly from the App Store.

Game and App of the Day

Apple's editors pick one game and app that is most exciting and deliver it to you every day. You just need to look at this tab.

Search

This tab makes it easy to find what you are interested in for instant search results. It includes tips and tricks, editorial stories, and lists.

7.2 Installing and Uninstalling Apps

Installing and uninstalling apps from App Store on Apple iPhone 11 Pro Max is straightforward.

Installing Apps

To install new apps, set up your iPhone for internet connection, and activate Apple ID on the phone. Follow these steps:

- o Go to the "App Store."
- o To find the app, tap on "Search."
- o Tap on the search field and key in the subject of the app you are looking for.
- o Enter "search."
- o Select the required app.
- o Go back to the home screen.
- o Uninstall Apps

You can uninstall apps anytime to free up your phone's memory.

Uninstall App

o Tap and hold any app.
o Select "Rearrange Apps."
o Tap on "Delete."
o Go back to the home screen.
o Using this method, app settings and the relevant data will be deleted from the phone memory.

Uninstall App without Deleting Data

o Go to "Settings."
o Tap on "General."
o Go to "iPhone Storage."
o Tap on the required app.
o Go to the "Offload App."
o Go back to the home screen.
o By using this method, the app data will not be deleted from the phone memory.

7.3 App Store Settings

Some crucial settings for the App Store have been given below:

Settings to Refresh Background Apps on iPhone 11 Pro Max

When you go back to the phone's home screen, some apps keep running in the background. By setting your phone to refresh those apps, you can still see notifications without even that app is active.

- Go to "Background App Refresh"
- Select "Settings."
- Go to "General."
- Go to "Background App Refresh."

To turn this feature on or off:

- Select "Background App Refresh."
- Tap on the "On" or "Off" tab.

To turn on this feature using Wi-Fi:

- Go to "Wi-Fi."
- If you activate this feature using your Wi-Fi, then the content of the app will automatically be updated whenever Wi-Fi connection is available and established.

To turn on this feature using your mobile network:

- Go to "Wi-Fi & Mobile Data."
- If you turn on this feature using your Wi-Fi, then the app content will be updated even when a Wi-Fi connection is not present.

Turning On Unused Apps

You can also set your iPhone to delete apps you have not been using. You can do this to free up the phone memory. App data and settings will be saved and restored whenever you plan to reinstall the app. To do this, follow these steps:

- Go to the "iTunes & App Store."

o Tap on "Settings."
o Go to the "iTunes & App Store."
o Tap on the indicator right next to the "Offload Unused Apps" tap to turn this feature on/off.

Update Apps Setting

With iOS 13 in iPhone 11 Pro Max, the apps downloaded from the App Store are updated by default. You will not get any notifications about updates. But if you want to, you can always go and update apps manually. If you like to do it manually, you can always turn off automatic updates. By downloading an app on one phone, it will not be automatically installed on your other phone. But if you want all of your purchased apps to be downloaded on all of your iPhones, there is an option of turning on the "Automatic Downloads." Before beginning, ensure that you have the latest version of iOS, then log in to all of your iPhones with the same Apple ID.

Updating Apps Manually

o Go to the "App Store."
o Tap "Today."
o Select your profile icon.
o Scroll down to find out any pending updates.
o Go to "Update" right next to the app, or press "Update All."

Turning "On" or "Off" Automatic Updates

- Select "Settings."
- Tap on your name.
- Go to the "iTunes & App Store."
- Turn on or off "App Updates." If you shut down automatic updates, you still receive notifications from the App Store whenever an app's update is released.

Chapter 8: Notes and Reminders Settings

This chapter will cover the features and settings of the Notes and Reminders Apps in the iPhone 11 Pro Max. With iOS 13 as its operating system, iPhone 11 Pro Max gives you much more flexibility and some new exciting features.

8.1 Notes Settings

The Notes App on iPhone 11 Pro Max is an incredible method to remain sorted out. You can likewise impart notes to companions or sync over various gadgets utilizing iCloud. Notwithstanding how you use Notes, it might be needed to change settings to customize it. The iOS 13 update naturally changed Notes, to begin with, a huge, intense title. iOS 13 accompanies various new highlights alongside some other forms of old highlights. So whether you get the iPhone 11, or either the 11 Pro or 11 Pro Max, there is a bounty to find.

Creating a New Note on iPhone 11 Pro Max

To create a new note on iPhone 11 Pro Max, go to the Notes App, which you can see on your iPhone's home screen. Tap on the "Create a New Note" button. Tap inside the note and start writing.

Then tap "Done" to save your note. In this way, you will exit the editing mode. You can create another one by tapping the "New Note" button.

Editing an Existing Note on iPhone 11 Pro Max

To edit an existing note, go to the Notes App on your iPhone. Select the note you want to edit by tapping anywhere inside the note and start updating/editing. Tap "Done" when you are satisfied to save the changes.

Moving a Note to another folder

You can move a note anytime if you think it should be in another folder or if you just want to put in a new folder. Just go to the Notes App on your iPhone. Select the folder in which the note is. Tap the "Select Notes". Choose the note that you want to move in another folder. Select "Move To" option. Then, simply choose the folder where you want to move the note. Tap "New Folder" if you want a new folder.

Deleting a Note

To delete a note that you do not want anymore, simply go to the Notes App. Select the note. Select the "Trash" button. If you want to make it quick, swipe right to left, and tap the "Delete" button. This will send the note to a folder named "Recently Deleted" for one month, after which the note will be permanently deleted

New Features in Notes App in iPhone 11 Pro Max

Following are some of the exciting new features in iPhone 11 Pro Max with iOS 13 operating system:

New Gallery View

It has a new gallery view. If the note primarily contains text, you will see that in the thumbnail. If a note has a sketch or picture, it will take up the edge. It is a slick method to see your notes and locate the one that you are searching for.

Folders Can Be Moved

In iOS 12 and prior versions, organizers were fixed set up. Presently, you can move them, as much you might want. Either simply press-hold a folder or a sub-folder from the fundamental Folders page and drag it where you need it, or pick "Move This Folder,"

Sub-Folders are available on iPhone 11 Pro Max

You would now be able to add subfolders to your organizers in the Notes aApp. Drag a folder on the head of another to transform the first folder into a sub-folder.

Better Sorting Options for Notes in Folders

You would now be able to sort notes in singular folders legitimately in-app. Previously, these choices were just accessible in the "Settings" app and would apply to the entirety of your folders. Presently, if you need to sort one folder's notes by "Title," another by "Date Edited," and another by "Date Created," you can do that here. Simply swipe down remaining in a folder and tap the "Sort by ..." and drop-down.

Useful Tips for Using Notes App on iPhone 11 Pro Max

o   You can easily create a list of to-dos on the Notes app. Just go to Notes app and pick "New Checklist."

o   The most effective method to share and work together on the Notes app is to add as many people as you want by tapping the Plus (+) sign. By doing so, you can include contacts who can view or make changes continuously.

o   You can turn on passwords in Notes. Just go to "Settings", and select "Notes" — tap "Password". Here you can set a default secret key for every one of your notes, and you can empower Face ID as well.

o   You can also lock a note. Open Notes. Tap "Lock Note" in the drop-down menu. Presently type in your secret key, and it will be bolted. You can likewise do it by opening a note, squeezing the offer symbol, and afterwards, the "Lock Note" symbol. That only adds the lock symbol to the note. Tap on the symbol to bolt the note. Next time when you get to it, you will require the secret phrase.

8.2 Reminder Settings

We would all be able to be distracted. Regardless of whether it is a staple rundown, undertakings for a significant venture, or only making sure to send a few messages and make a few calls Now and then we overlook some important things on our plan for the day. Fortunately for all of us, the Reminders app is ideal for helping you remember the assignments you need to finish. You can set up planned occasions for your iPhone to help you remember certain undertakings. You can get your iPhone to help you remember a specific errand when you leave or enter an area, and you can even set suggestions to rehash so you can make sure to accomplish something month to month, week by week, or even every day.

Creating a Reminder on iPhone 11 Pro Max

Follow these steps to create, edit, and delete any reminder:

- From the Home screen of your iPhone 11 Pro Max, choose "Reminders App"
- Choose "New Reminder" to create a new reminder and give it a name.
- Set a date for the reminder by scrolling up and down.
- Set a time for the reminder by scrolling up and down.
- Choose a reminder alert.
- Choose the "Repeat" option if you want to repeat a reminder by itself.
- Choose an option.
- To set the reminder for a specific location, enter a location, and follow the instructions given on-screen.
- Tap "Done".
- The reminder has been created and saved.
- Check the reminder to mark as completed.

The Reminders app is not one of the most popular implicit apps, generally because of its restricted usefulness in examination with other updates and to-do apps accessible from the App Store. In iOS 13, Apple updated the Reminders app's interface, including another look and new capacities that may urge more individuals to look at it. Let's have a look:

New Design of Reminders App

iOS 12 and older versions had a simple list-style view. Items were organized by list, but the new operating system, iOS 13,has a new interface that is more interesting. There are four main sections in Reminders App, which organize all of your family and work reminders in one view so you can see them easily. "Today" section is there for reminders that demand urgent attention, a "Scheduled" section is there for reminders attached to a date.

An "All" section is there for viewing everything in one view and all at once, and a "Flagged" section for reminders uses a flag to separate them from other reminders. Apart from having these four main sections that offer an organized view to see all your reminders, you can also find your reminders organized using the "My Lists" section.

You can have many lists. You can separate your lists for family, work, friends, or as per any criteria. The Reminders app will handle all of your household chores. Tap on the "Add List" button to add a new list. All of your lists will be shown in the "My Lists" section. You can also find the individual list easily. To add a reminder to a particular list can be done by selecting a list and tapping on the "New Reminder" section.

More Customized Options

The Reminders app in iPhone 11 Pro Max gives you new customization options for your Reminders list-making. There are some additional colors and new icons. You can choose colors of your choice and give your lists new icons like work, food, etc. to provide them with a more visual appeal.

When you create a reminder in iPhone 11 Pro Max, you will see a quick access toolbar through which you can add locations, times, and much more to your reminders. You can choose any icon to make your reminder more feasible and useful for you.

- o Icon "Clock" will allow you to schedule a reminder. It may be for today, this weekend, or any custom date.
- o There is another icon "Arrow" that will allow you to set the activation time when you arrive or leave any custom location or get in or out of the car. You can choose your location.
- o "Flag" allows you to put a flag on a reminder so you can easily find it later.
- o "Camera" lets you take and add a photo to a reminder. There is a new feature of adding attachments to your reminders.

You can put your reminders in a repeat mode. You can access all of the options available in reminders by tapping on the "Custom" button. You can do so while creating a new reminder or editing an existing one. Interface in the "Reminders" App in iPhone 11 Pro Max is simpler and makes it easier to use.

Making a Group of Lists in the Reminders App

You can make a group of separate reminders lists, and give them a single heading in your Reminders app. If you have a list of your favorite things or places, you can combine them into a group, and give it a name. It offers a better organization that you can see in the "My Lists" section.

- o To add a new group, just tap on "Edit" and then select the "Add Group" option. You can also choose to drag and drop the option to arrange your lists.
- o When you use the "Drag and Drop" option, you can simply drag a reminder under another to form a nested reminder in your reminders list. By doing so, you can add small tasks under a large reminder. For example, you can create a reminder for shopping; you might also add more specific and smaller reminders like medicines, shoes, etc. You need to go to the "All Reminders" section if you want

to use the "Drag and Drop" option to rearrange reminders lists.

Sharing a Reminders List in iPhone 11 Pro Max

There is a tap option of three dots (...) in the upper right corner of any reminders list in the "Reminders" App. You can let another person see the changes made to the list. You need to add that person. Although this option was already there, in iPhone 11 Pro Max, its location is changed in redesigning this app.

Enhanced Siri Intelligence

Reminders features have improved Siri's intelligence in iPhone 11 Pro Max. You can now type a more descriptive and longer sentence. Reminders will understand them very well and will also give suggestions. For example, you are talking to someone in Messages, and mention having lunch tomorrow, Siri will provide you with a suggestion to create a reminder for that.

Changing Reminder Alert

- To change the reminders alert in iPhone 11 Pro Max, go to "Settings" from the home screen.
- Select Sounds & Haptics to set a ringtone. You can pick "Reminder Alert" from the list of available ringtones and select your favorite one by scrolling through it.
- Reminders alert sound has been set up.

Chapter 9: iTunes Store and Apple Books App

This chapter will discuss the features and settings of the iTunes app and the Books app in the iPhone 11 Pro Max. We will also learn some tips on tackling some issues for the smooth working of these apps.

9.1 iTunes Store Settings

You can enjoy movies, music, TV shows, and much more on your iPhone through the iTunes store. You will need an Apple ID and Internet connection to use the iTunes Store. You have two options; Browse or Search. Browse what you are not sure of what you have been looking for by category or genre. Select the category and then tap "Genre" to refine your list better. If you are assured of what you are looking for, enter your information into the search field and simply tap Search, or you can watch what is trending. When you have the "Family Sharing" option turned on, you can enjoy, download or simply view TV shows, songs, or movies that have been purchased by your family members. Tap "Purchased", then tap your name, and then choose a family member.

Let's look at some settings that you can do to the iTunes store app:

- o For setting options for the iTunes Store, you need to go to "Settings" and tap "iTunes & App Store".
- o To view or edit your account, go to your "Apple ID". To change your password, the "Password" tap is available to make any changes.
- o You can also sign in using another Apple ID. You need to sign out of your previous Apple ID and sign in with a different Apple ID.
- o You can also turn on or off the automatic download options.
- o You can also use Siri to search and make purchases or download in the iTunes Store. You can also buy it later in the "Siri" tab. For example, you can tap Movies, then tap "Siri" to have a list of movies available for download or purchase. You can also add items to your "Wish List", something that you hope to purchase from the iTunes Store, you simply need to tap "Add to Wish List".
- o You can choose your favorite buttons. You can rearrange these buttons. Tap "More" then go to "Edit". Drag the icon you want to replace with another icon, then tap "Done".

Fixing iPhone 11 Pro Max not Recognized in iTunes

iTunes assumes an imperative job with including new iOS substances with constant improvement. To utilize iTunes on the iPhone, you should introduce it on a good PC first. You can associate iPhone 11 Pro Max to use an Apple-provided USB/Lightning link to the PC. If you can see no issue involving USB ports, and connection/connector, iTunes ought to have the option to distinguish your iPhone right away. Else, you will need to preclude singular factors that may have impeded the association. The solutions have been given below to fix an issue on the iPhone 11 Pro Max not working in iTunes.

Peruse on to discover why this occurs and causing your iOS gadget to match up with iTunes. Retry matching up iPhone 11 Pro Max in the wake of playing out every one of the accompanying strategies:

Restart your iPhone

To dispense with arbitrary iOS issues that may have destroyed the synchronizing procedure between your iTunes and iOS gadget, reboot your iPhone. Before doing so, make sure to disengage the lightning link from the PC's USB port. When it is separated, follow these means to delicately reset your iPhone.

Tap and hold "Volume Up" catches for a couple of moments. Discharge the two catches when the bar showing "Slide to Power off" shows up— then swipe the bar in order to shut down your gadget. After around 25 seconds, you need to tap and hold Side catch and afterward discharge when the logo of Apple shows up. Trust that your iPhone will get done with resetting, and once it is fully operational, retry interfacing it with the iTunes then check whether iTunes is currently ready to remember it.

Deactivate restrictions on iPhone

When empowered, restrictions on iPhone might likewise confine it from getting to iTunes administrations. To wipe out this from the primary causes, attempt to debilitate restrictions on iPhone 11 Pro Max in order to remove all app restrictions.

Simply follow these instructions:

- o Go to "Settings" from the Home screen.
- o At that point, click on "Screen Time".
- o Choose Content and Privacy Restrictions.

Resetting all the Settings

To get out of some customization or settings on your gadget, the option of resetting all the settings will help. It will eradicate all your present settings, including tweaked data.

Any mistakes related to invalid settings will likewise be wiped out. If you want to attempt it, at that point you can allude to these means:

- o Tap on "Settings"
- o Go to "General"
- o Click on "Reset"
- o Click on "Reset All the Settings"
- o Enter your password.
- o Affirm activity by choosing "Reset All the Settings"

Update iTunes Store App

Staying up with the latest version is prescribed to guarantee security and smooth working. Furthermore, that idea applies to the iTunes app. To evade framework clashes, the most recent form of iTunes should be utilized. In case you do not know whether you are using the refreshed variant or not, follow these means to affirm. You have downloaded the iTunes from the official site of Apple; this is what you ought to do:

- o Go to "iTunes" on your PC.
- o Tap "Help"
- o Select "Check for Latest Updates"

o Proceed by following the on-screen orders to introduce the most recent rendition of iTunes accessible on your PC.

Remember to restart your PC in the wake of introducing essential programming refreshes. If you do this, it will guarantee that all framework changes are appropriately applied. When your PC reboots, dispatch the iTunes app at that point and interface your PC to the iPhone again to check whether iTunes has effectively remembered it.

9.2 Apple Books App Settings

Apple has completely remodeled the "iBooks" App into the "Apple Books" App with some significant changes in the older version iOS 12 and smaller ones, adding updates for iOS 13. Many users are finding it challenging to learn new features. With the change in name from "iBooks" to "Books", Apple has introduced a couple of design changes and other features that have brought "iBooks" close to other Apple apps like the "Podcasts" Apps or "TV". In the "Books" App in iPhone 11 Pro Max, you can organize and purchase books, change the brightness or fonts, and even take notes. The iPhone has also started showing the bookstore sections that include the options of "Books We Love" and "Coming Soon", and other genres like memoirs and biographies.

Finding and Buying your Favorite Books on Books App

On iPhone 11 Pro Max, Go to the "Books" App. Select the "Book Store". Browse the books that are on your top list. You can choose the Browse Sections to see various genres like Fiction or Nonfiction.

Organization of your Library

You can sort your PDFs and books alphabetically or you can drag them to make an arrangement to choose later on. On your iPhone, tap the "Library". Go to "Collections", then click the word next to the "Sort" button, select "Author", "Title", or "Manually"

Downloading a Book

In order to read an already purchased book even when you are not connected to the Internet, make sure you have downloaded it before going offline. To download the book, find it in your "Library". Go to the "Download" button. If you cannot find the "Download" button, it means that book has already been downloaded.

Discover Other Ways to Read

You can also listen to various audiobooks in the "Books" App on iPhone 11 Pro Max just like you can do on Apple Watch. You can take the help of Siri for audiobooks devices.

Fixing Apple Books App not recognized on Apple iPhone 11 Pro Max

If you love to read books or eBooks, then the Apple Books App is only for you. The Apple Books App works well on the iPhone. Using the "Books" App, you can have eBooks directly from the app on your iPhone. You will get access to all the collections based on best-selling categories, titles, fiction, non-fiction, authors, etc. Users can easily download and read their preferred eBooks.

You can also manage your Library, listen to various audiobooks, and more. An active internet connection should be there for smoother user experience. However, that is not the case every time. However, if you are facing issues with the "Books" App, check out solutions below and learn how to fix Apple Books not working on Apple iPhone 11 Pro Max.

Refresh Internet Connection

Check your internet connection, and see if it is properly working. Try to refresh it. Go to your "settings" and try refreshing your internet connection. Wait for a few seconds. Go to your "Books" App again and see if the problem is fixed. If it is still not working, then go to the next step.

Check Pending App Updates

Go to the "App Store" on your phone and look for a "User Profile" icon. You will automatically see the "Update" option right next to the app if there are any updates available. If they are available, then tap on the "Update" and wait for the process to complete. Go to the "Books" App again, and see if it is working fine.

Reset Network Settings

To get out of invalid settings or customization on your gadget, resetting network settings can help. This will eradicate all your present settings, including tweaked data. Any mistakes related to incorrect settings will likewise be wiped out. If you wish to attempt it, at that point you can allude to these means:

- o From the Home screen, tap on "Settings"
- o Select "General"
- o Tap on "Reset"
- o Tap "Reset Network Settings" from the given choices.
- o Enter your password.
- o Affirm activity by tapping on "Reset Network Settings"

Trust that your iPhone will complete the process of resetting. It will restart without anyone else when the reset is finished.

By then, you can begin empowering important highlights on your iPhone so you can utilize them again, not surprisingly.

Force Books App to Close and Restart

Swipe up at the bottom of your iPhone screen and then pause to open the app to see cards. Now, from the application switcher, explore the "Books Application Review". Swipe up the "Books Application Review Card" to close it forcefully. Then, reboot your handset and retry utilizing the Books App.

Remove Books App Restrictions

Restrictions on your iPhone may likewise confine it from getting to Books App administrations. To wipe out it from the underlying causes, attempt to debilitate restrictions on iPhone to lift all restrictions, including access to iTunes. Simply follow these instructions:

- o Tap "Settings"
- o At that point, tap on "Screen Time"
- o Select "Content" and "Privacy Restrictions"
- o

Have a go at associating your iPhone to the Books App again. At the same time, restrictions are debilitated. Check whether that makes some positive results if the Books App can recognize your gadget and re-empower restrictions.

Signing out and Signing in again in your Apple Account

On your home screen, go to "Settings". Then tap on the user account at the top. Sign out of your account. If it is demanding the password, then simply enter the password and sign out. After that, restart your phone. When the phone is functional again, sign in to your account. You can also add a different account to sign in and then access the Books app.

Offload Books App or Reinstall

From your home screen, go to the "Settings" menu, then tap on "General". From the options, choose "iPhone Storage". When you scroll down, you will find Books from the list. Select the "Offload App" button to free up the cache and other storage space. When it is done, restart your phone. Follow the same instructions to "Onload" the app again. You can also have the option of deleting the Books App from your phone and then reinstalling it.

Update the Software

If nothing is working to fix your device, you need to check for the latest software update. Go to the "Settings" on your iPhone. Tap "General", and then go to "Software Update".

It will automatically check if there are any latest iOS updates.

If they are available, you just need to make sure to download it and install it while having a Wi-Fi connection. When it is done, go to the Books App, and see if the problem is resolved.

Check the Time and Date

Ensure that the time and date on your gadget are set accurately for your time region. To fix this, on your iPhone, open the "Settings". Then tap "General", go to "Date and Time". Get more assistance with the date and time. In case if the date and time are off base, update them, and see if the problem is resolved.

Chapter 10: Use of Health App on iPhone 11 Pro Max

The Health app in iPhone 11 Pro Max gathers health-related data from your Apple Watch, your iPhone and other apps that you have already been using. So, you can view all information and track your progress at one place. The Health App automatically watches and counts your exercise distances. You can also enter data into different categories or just import it from other apps to your Health App. You will have to do activities every day to build your daily profile of a particular category like weight. Health App will make it more useful and it will simply note down your weight in some journals. The Health App gives you a prominent picture of your progress. You can have this process for different activities and metrics. In this chapter, we will learn the new feature that Apple has added in iPhone 11 Pro Max with iOS 13, how you can make the best out of your Health App, collecting and sharing your health-related data, and setting up a Medical ID.

10.1 Health App - An Overview

Apple's Health App, which is shown with iOS 13, permits you to screen your fitness and well-being status, make essential data accessible to get in shape, and track your fitness and health routine. Apple has added new and exciting features and functionality to its apps, which are worth noting. In iOS 12 interface, there are four tabs:

- o Today calendar
- o Health Data
- o Sources
- o Medical ID

The Health app in iPhone 11 Pro Max having iOS 13 has just two tabs i.e.

- o Summary
- o Browse

Summary Tab

It gives you an overview of the different health related data, which varies based on other health-related devices that you use. Data like your activity, variability in heart rate, blood pressure can also be displayed in your "Health App". You can easily edit your data by only going to the "Summary" tab.

Then go to "Edit" and simply tap the categories related to your health that you want to see. The "Summary" App also has a "Highlights" tab that tells you exciting and relevant information like your workout minutes over the last week, daily average steps walked, and much more. Towards the end of the "Summary" tab section, there are options like Registration for Organ Donation. There is also other health-related information and for understanding the health issues.

Browse Tab

In the "Browse" Tab, you can find a list of health-related categories. It makes it easier to find health information related to categories you are interested in. It makes it less hectic for you to find out the information you have been looking for. Let's look at some of the other prominent features of the Health App:

o In the "Profile" section, which is available when you tap on your profile picture on the "Health" App, you can find your medical ID information. In this section, you can also limit other devices and apps that can access your health information available on the Health App. You can keep your health records in this section. It also has your health details like age, height, weight, etc.

o Health app was used to be organized by date but is no longer held like that in its new features. By tapping a health category, you might see a different look like exercise minutes. Data can still be organized by day, week, or month. But it is easier to find a category.

o A new health tracking feature is there for you, which is tracking menstrual cycles. As compared to other apps, it gives you more privacy. It can monitor both periods and fertility. It keeps track of data like when expected, period history, and different symptoms and patterns related to periods and fertility.

o iOS 13 continually monitors the noise level. Through the Health App, it can send notifications whenever there are harmful noise levels around you, like if there is a loud concert or loud music while using headphones, Apple instantly informs you through the Health App, and recommends an acceptable level suitable for your ears.

o If you have a toothbrush data on another app, Health App can import that data to keep track of your toothbrush time or you can add data manually in your Health app. Then it will keep track and let you know when you need to brush your teeth.

How to Use Your Health App to Make the Best out of it

To make the best out of your health app, take into account the following tips:

Start with Single Category

Start with only one activity, whether it is your activity, adjusting your eating routine, and getting more rest. It is essentially difficult to make a massive difference simultaneously, even though that is what you should do. Instead, adopt a gentler strategy and simply tackle one zone that needs improvement. Odds are there but one new sound propensity will prompt others after some time.

Do not Hesitate to Have Professional Help

In case you are genuinely attempting to translate your Health information, or entirely do not have the foggiest idea how to manage it, address a doctor or enrolled dietitian to get some assistance. Fitness coaches and well-being mentors can likewise assist you in moving on the information in your Health app.

Make Top Choices

You do not have to consider the entirety of the information that health supplies you with; there is no utilization bouncing around here and there. You can put explicit information focused on the top choices tab on the principal page of the app.

To do this, basically find the information point you need to top pick and tap the slider that says, "Add to top choices."

You can do this for the same number of information focuses as you like so that you can concentrate on the information you require and overlook the rest.

10.2 Collect and Share Health Data

Apple is exceptionally quick to stress how profoundly it organizes your privacy. Information in the Health App is scrambled both on your gadgets and on Apple's servers, and if you have two-factor validation turned for you, not even Apple can take a gander at the well-being logs you have developed. You can peruse Apple's privacy strategy, yet you should likewise examine the different administrations' security strategies you connect up with Apple Health. To see which apps are presently associated with Apple Health, open the app on your gadget, tap your symbol in the upper right corner, and pick Apps under Privacy.

Note that the authorizations on the following screen will be part of composing consents — the app can add information to Apple Health — and read consents, which implies that the app can take and use information from Apple Health.

You have the alternative to handicap any authorizations, detach the app totally, and completely erase all the information that the app has gathered—at any rate as far as what has been imparted to Apple Health. Talking about erasing information, pick "Devices" from the past menu. At that point, pick a gadget from the rundown, and with a few taps, you can delete everything Apple Health hangs on you. You can likewise erase singular records, as opposed to everything simultaneously, by choosing the individual classes recorded.

There is no ace setting to stop Apple Health gathering information from your gadgets once you have turned it on. However, you can adequately stop it by obstructing its entrance to the sensors in your iPhone. From iOS "Settings", tap "Privacy", at that point, turn off the "Fitness Tracking" choice. Try to enter your data. On the off chance that the parameter is in your "Dashboard", simply tap it there. At that point, tap "Add Data Point". Something else, tap Health Data at the base of the screen, tap the parameter you need to refresh, at that point tap "Add Data Point".

10.3 Create a Medical ID

Your iPhone can show significant contact and medical data on the "Lock screen", where it is accessible for somebody taking care of you in an emergency. Anyone who has access to your iPhone can peruse the data you remember for your emergency Medical ID. To set up your Medical ID, follow the instructions:

o When you open this app, you get a welcome screen. You must include essential data-name, sexual orientation, and date of birth, weight, and height.

o Afterward, you are brought to the "Summary" screen, which gives you an overview of your present insights, contingent upon what you need to know. One of the first things you might need to do is to set up medical data for specialists on call.

o At the point, when you initially go into the Health App, you will have to set up your Medical ID. Tap on the profile picture; you will find the "Medical Details" option there, then tap on the "Medical ID" option.

o Enter any ailments, hypersensitivities, meds you take, and blood classification; you can likewise include an emergency contact from your contact list.

o That point onward, when you tap on the "Emergency Connect" on your password screen, you would not just have the option to make an emergency call. Yet, you will additionally approach medical data and emergency contact information.

- When you have begun utilizing the Health app, you can alter, add to, or simply see your medical data by tapping on the "Profile" section on the "Summary" screen. You can likewise change the privacy settings for any gadgets you may have associated with the Health App.

- Utilize the Health App to monitor your fitness and health data. Enter data for key parameters, or let the Health App gather data from different apps and gadgets that screen your well-being and action. You can even impart explicit data to choose apps.

To edit emergency contacts, follow the instructions:

- Go to the "Health App" and then go to the "Summary" tab.
- Tap on your "Profile" picture.
- Under the option of "Medical Details", go to "Medical ID".
- Go to "Edit", and then to "Emergency Contacts".

o To add a contact and your relationship with that contact, tap the Plus button, which you will find next to "Add Emergency Contact." On the other hand, to remove a contact, go to the "Delete" button next to that contact you want to exclude.

Conclusion

The iPhone 11 Pro Max has pushed everything up to a notch. Having a great display and a new camera has enhanced its attraction. It is an expensive device as compared to the previous models, but it is a great phone. The iPhone 11 Pro Max is much similar to the iPhone XS Max in design. But the main visual difference is the addition of a frosted glass finish and an extra camera on the rear. The front of this iPhone features an improved OLED display, and Face ID. Within the frosted glass back of this phone, a square camera protrusion features three camera lenses. Interestingly, the back of this iPhone is made up of the same piece of glass.

The iPhone 11 Pro Max is at the top of its game. As compared to the iPhone 8 or the iPhone XS, the specifications of this phone are monstrous. This indicates that Apple is pushing hard to maintain dominance in the flagship space. The camera on this phone is a striking feature. The three cameras set up is really impressive. The features like Portrait Mode have shown a drastic improvement. It is a complete package. The rest of the phone features are also impressive and convincing. It is the camera features that shine the most.

iPhone 11 Pro Max has iOS 13.0 operating system. This phone has a power source of the Hexa Core processor. It has 64 GB internal storage and 4 GB RAM. It has also got the Apple A13 Bionic Chipset. What a fantastic combination of technology!

Apple has always a pack of amazing built-in apps that are integral for the smooth functioning of your iPhone and enhance your user experience. Apps like Video Chat, Apple's iMessage, the Calendar App, FaceTime, and many more are there to make your day. This book has discussed the features and settings of some of the most useful and crucial ones. But you can search through a vast collection of some fantastic apps as per your interests and taste. These cool features make this iPhone great. But the highlight of this phone is camera and the battery life.

There are some other amazing features in iPhone 11 Pro Max, like Face ID that is the most secure way to operate your phone through facial authentication. It is easier to use with having improved performance even at varying distances. It supports many angles. Spatial audio in iPhone 11 Pro Max provides a fantastic sound experience. Apple is trying to uplift its level with new iPhone designs. It has always been doing so and this phone is one of the proofs of their best possible vision.

By going through this book, you must have learned how to set up your iPhone 11 Pro Max, how to activate your Apple ID which you need to operate this phone, and Face ID, iCloud, and some tips regarding iOS 13. You must have also learned the settings of some basic and most crucial apps like Messages, Email, iMessaging, Calls and Contacts, the Camera app, the App Store, the Notes and Reminders App, the iTunes App, and the Books App in the iPhone 11 Pro Max. You must have also learned some tips on tackling some issues related to the use of your iPhone 11Pro Max. Hopefully, this book will serve as a guide to learn about all your queries related to the use of the new iPhone 11Pro Max.

Made in the USA
Middletown, DE
10 October 2023

40587628R00084